"When did we see You?"

DEDICATION

To Mae D. and William Schutt, Mathilda M. and John D. Voss, Leonard S. and Betty J. Tromp . . . aunts and uncles who have shared God's love with me! (PVW)

In memory of Mary McDaniel Aalsburg, a student of the Bible, who saw Jesus in "the least of these" and knitted thousands of mittens for those with cold hands, prepared hundreds of meals for those new to the United States, distributed countless loaves of bread to those without work, wrote regular letters encouraging many who labored in foreign countries, and shared her home with all in need of her hospitality. (CAW)

"When did we see You?"

Sixty Creative Activities to Help
Fourth to Eighth Graders
Recognize Jesus Today

PHYLLIS VOS WEZEMAN
COLLEEN AALSBURG WIESSNER

AVE MARIA PRESS
NOTRE DAME, INDIANA 46556

© 1994 by Ave Maria Press, Inc., Notre Dame, IN 46556

International Standard Book Number: 0-87793-535-1

Library of Congress Catalog Card Number: 94-71582

Cover, text design and illustrations by Katherine Robinson Coleman

Photography: Gail Denham 64; Marilyn Nolt 10, 36, 86, 108; Steve & Mary Skjold 132.

Cover photographs: left and right — Steve & Mary Skjold Photographs; middle — Marilyn Nolt.

Printed and bound in the United States of America.

Contents

FOUR
I was poor 87

FIVE
I was sick 109

SIX
I was imprisoned 133

Introduction

Who are the **hungry**?

Could she be the elderly woman living on your street who can no longer get out to the market on her own?

Who are the **thirsty**?

Could he be the young adolescent yearning for God to help him make sense of his life?

Who are the **strangers**?

Could she be the new girl at school who has just moved to the area with her family?

Who are the **poor**?

Could they be the family whose possessions and home were destroyed in the overnight fire?

Who are the **sick**?

Could he be the teen-ager who seeks to control his low self-image by eating either the wrong foods or not enough at all.

Who are the **imprisoned**?

Could she be the young girl suffering from the pain of sexual abuse?

Jesus concluded a long discourse recorded in the gospel of Matthew with a parable of a king who judged his subjects based on how they treated one another. In fact, the king told his people, "Truly I tell you, just as you did it to one of the least of these who are members of my family, you did it to me." Christians have always taken this to mean that by sharing God's love with the "least of these," they are doing it for Jesus.

The difficulty in this teaching often comes in finding these least ones. Often, the teaching seems so abstract. Who really knows someone who is physically hungry? Who really knows someone who has been jailed? The learning activities in *"When Did We See You?"* will help young people to find Jesus in the people of their daily lives and experience. By looking at these six questions in a new light, the participants will be helped to a clearer understanding of the least ones and their needs. They will realize that each day everyone comes into contact with someone who falls into one of these categories. Through recognizing these people, meeting their needs, and sharing God's love, the young people will find out what it is like to come face to face with Jesus Christ.

Called the parable of the last judgment, the story of the king and his subjects is only ten verses long, yet Matthew 25:35–45 provides a concise synopsis of themes such as justice, love in action, and faithfulness which are woven throughout the Bible. Even the location of this passage carries an important message. In the same discourse, Jesus also shares the parable of the ten bridesmaids, a message that reminds his followers of his imminent return, and the parable of the talents, which tells Christians that their God-given talents must be multiplied for the good of others and of God's kingdom. In both parables we are told how to use our time before Jesus returns.

In Matthew 25:35–45, Jesus is even more specific. He presents a clear model of discipleship. We are reminded that Christ is always with us, sometimes disguised as those around us who need our help. Most importantly, these are not tasks for the highly skilled or the uniquely called, they are something which every follower can and must do in the name of Christ. Since Jesus would no longer be on earth with the disciples, he wanted to make it clear that good deeds done for others were the same as kindnesses expressed directly to him.

The six chapters of *"When Did We See You?"* each contain ten learning activities which explore one aspect of the chapter's theme. Each lesson plan is organized into three parts. A *learn* section presents a description of the theme of the activity and describes what the students will do. A *locate* column provides a list of needed supplies and other advance preparations to do before beginning the learning activity. The *lead* section details the directions for successfully guiding a group through the activity. Although each lesson is related to the passage, Matthew 25:35–45, it is also organized around another story or verse from the Bible which further illustrates the specific topic.

Sharing God's love was a task not only given to the disciples thousands of years ago, it is the responsibility of every Christian today. *"When Did We See You?"* provides creative, concrete, challenging methods for responding to Jesus' commission. It once again challenges each and every learner with the question "What will you do?"

ONE

I was hungry

Overview

Over and over again the Bible tells of God's concern for those who are hungry. At creation God provided everything people needed in order to live. It is only after Adam and Eve sinned that people had to struggle to survive and to work hard to meet their needs. Isaiah 55:1 proclaims the day when people will be able to "come, buy and eat . . . without money and without price." The image of heaven as a banquet reveals God's ideal. Even the poor, the lame, and the outcast will have a place at God's table.

Throughout salvation history God provided food for people in miraculous ways. The manna in the wilderness (Ex 16:4-35) and the feeding of the five thousand (Mk 6:34-44) are just two examples. God also provided food through faithful servants who put love into action by caring for those who were hungry. They were commended for their justice and kindness. In the parable of the last judgment, Jesus said of these people "Just as you did it to one of the least of these who are members of my family, you did it to me" (Mt 25:40).

This chapter examines three types of hunger which are present both in the biblical stories and in the world today. The activities in this chapter will help the participants explore causes, effects, and solutions of physical, emotional, and spiritual hunger. They will discover what it means to feed those who are hungry, meeting their needs in the name of Jesus.

Working for Justice

HAPPY ARE THOSE WHO GIVE FOOD TO THE HUNGRY.

Psalm 146:7

LEARN

There are many ways in which a person can be involved in the church as it "executes justice for the oppressed [and] gives food to the hungry" (Ps 146:7). Hunger programs through local congregations and organizations are supported through the efforts of people who give food, money, and time. However, many people still need to know how they can help. In this activity the participants will learn some of the ways Christians help to feed the hungry. They will communicate the problem of physical hunger to their local faith community and make a banner to advertise a program or need related to this theme.

LOCATE

- ✎ Natural-colored burlap bag, or brown grocery bags
- ✎ Labels from cans and jars
- ✎ Food bags, wrappers, and boxes
- ✎ Thick markers (dark colors)

- ✎ Scissors
- ✎ Glue
- ✎ Tape
- ✎ Information on one or more local food programs or agencies

LEAD

Ask the participants to name ways in which their church, school, or organization helps to feed the hungry (for example, through volunteering at a soup kitchen, collecting food for gift baskets, or raising money for a disaster relief fund). Share any additional information as needed.

Next, help the participants to understand the many necessary steps involving people and actions which are needed to feed the hungry. Ask: "How do you think the food gets from the people who donate it to the people who need it?" Act out the process with the participants, using some actual food items. Roles could include, for example:

◇ people who donate food or money to pay for food;

◇ people who package food for delivery;

◇ people who drive food to the program;

◇ people who unpack food and organize it for distribution;

◇ people who provide space for the food to be stored and distributed;

◇ people who distribute the food;

◇ people who come to the program to receive food which they need;

◇ people who clean and maintain the distribution area.

Read Psalm 146:7 to the group. Discuss how this verse relates to feeding the hungry. Ask: "What can you do to help people to become aware of the hungry in your own community? How can you invite more people to help feed the hungry?"

Next provide information to the group about a specific need. An agency may be in need of food to distribute, volunteers to work at the distribution center, or money to purchase special items. Tell the group that they are going to make one or more banners to advertise the need or needs of a local hunger relief agency.

A burlap bag, a piece of burlap, or brown grocery bags which have been taped together can be used as the background for a banner. Have the participants decorate the banner(s) in one of several ways:

1. Make a collage using the outer packaging from food; labels from cans or jars, wrappers, bags, or box surfaces can all be arranged on the banner and then glued or taped in place. Write the message or information in dark permanent marker across the surface of the collage.

2. Draw outlines of letters on labels and wrappers using thick, dark-colored marker. Cut out the letters, leaving the dark borders so that the letters will stand out clearly. Tape or glue in place on the banner.

3. Use labels and wrappers to make a border around the edges of the banner. For the message, use more labels or plain paper cut into letters to write a headline that describes the agency's need.

Provide the necessary materials. Assign or suggest one of the ideas. Allow the group time to create the banner(s).

Close the session by gathering in a circle around the completed banner(s). Pray for the needs of the people described. Hang the banner(s) in the church or another prominent place where they will be seen by many people from the congregation.

Dispelling the Myths

"I DESIRE MERCY AND NOT SACRIFICE."

Matthew 12:7

LEARN

It would seem that most people would want to do something to help combat the problem of world hunger. Unfortunately, many people have been misinformed about the issue. This misinformation leads to several false myths about the hunger crisis. When these myths are not addressed people become complacent and often refuse to offer their assistance. In this activity, the difference between myth and reality as related to the issue of hunger will be uncovered.

LOCATE

✎ Copies of Resource 1A, "Myths and Realities"

✎ Paper

✎ Pens or pencils

✎ Markers or crayons

LEAD

There are many common misconceptions, or myths, about world hunger. Distribute a copy of Resource 1A, "Myths and Realities," to each participant. Use one of the following methods to explore the five myths listed on the worksheet with the participants:

1. Assign individuals or small groups one myth and reality statement. Ask them to read and research more information on the issue and then report their findings to the entire group.
2. Have the participants make posters, overhead transparencies, or slides depicting each myth or reality statement. Have them use their project as a starting point for a debate on the issue.
3. Invite speakers from food relief agencies to dispel myths and present the facts on the hunger issue to the group.

To apply the lesson, have the participants each write fairy tales for one myth and one reality. You may wish to share the following examples, or create similar samples with the group.

Myth #1

There is not enough food for everyone in the world.

Sample Fairy Tale

Once there was a king who loved to eat. One day he wondered, "What if I would eat so much that I would run out of all of my favorite foods?" The king decided that would make him very sad. He called together his palace servants and told them to build walls around all of the fields and factories where food was grown and manufactured. Although the king continued to share food with his loyal subjects, he made sure that no one else would be able to have what now belonged to him.

Reality

There is enough food for everyone, however, it isn't distributed effectively, mainly because people who are hungry are also poor and can't afford it.

Sample Fairy Tale

Once there was a king who loved to eat. One day he wondered, "What if I would eat so much that I would run out of all of my favorite foods?" The king decided that it was not fair for him to have more and better food than everyone else, or to eat so much that others might not have enough food. So, he called together all of his servants and sent them out to see if the subjects of the land had enough to eat. The king began an education program in all of the schools and organizations to remind people to care for everyone and to be wise about what they ate. Then he called together a meeting of all the other kings of the world to figure out a plan to make sure that there would always be enough food for all of the kingdoms.

Distribute paper and pens or pencils for the project. Call on volunteers to share their fairy tales with the entire class. If you wish to extend the activity, have the students illustrate their fairy tales. Collect them together in one book.

Hungering for Happiness

"BLESSED ARE THOSE WHO HUNGER AND THIRST FOR RIGHTEOUSNESS, FOR THEY WILL BE FILLED."

Matthew 5:6

LEARN

In the words of the fifth beatitude Jesus explained that people hunger for happiness and satisfaction that comes from righteousness much in the same way that others hunger for food. In this activity, the participants will create and present a television-style talk show that discusses many of the different ways that people search for happiness. They will discover some of the ways that God provides happiness to those who experience a hunger for what is right.

LOCATE

- ✎ Stools or comfortable chairs
- ✎ End table or other setting props (optional)
- ✎ Prop microphone
- ✎ Clipboard (optional)
- ✎ Props for commercials (optional)
- ✎ Game show sign (optional)

LEAD

Read Matthew 5:6. Ask the participants to explain what they think the word "righteousness" means. Add your own information to enrich the definition. For example, righteousness means "acting in a just, upright manner; doing what is right, proper, or fitting." Ask: "What is one way that God wants you to act?" Call on volunteers to respond.

Ask the students if they have ever watched morning or afternoon television talk shows. Mention some of the hopeless dilemmas and life situations that are often presented on these programs. Compare the hunger and thirst for righteousness to the hunger and thirst which is often seen on talk shows. Ask: "Why do you think people watch television programs that usually portray hopeless topics? Who is responsible for this type of programming? What can be done to improve the quality of television talk shows and other programming?" Allow time for responses.

Tell the group that they are going to produce their own talk show. The topic of the program will be the search for happiness. A promotional teaser might be "I'll Just Be Happy If . . . Seekers of Happiness Tell Their Own Stories about the Search!" Or, the group might suggest its own title for the production. Assign roles like host, guests, crew, and members of the audience.

Allow time for preparation. The "guests" should prepare responses to questions in the areas of fame, money, success, education, and relationships. The "host" should quiz the guests about how these things can and cannot provide happiness. Each interview might end with the question, "Are you happy?" Instruct the guest to answer that question, "No, not yet, but I'll keep trying."

If time permits, allow the group to produce commercial advertisements that can be included in the presentation. Stay with the theme. Have the participants develop commercials related to a product or experience that offers happiness.

Create a set for the show. Stools or chairs can be arranged in a setting conducive to conversation. All the "guests" can sit on chairs "on stage" or they can be called one at a time from the audience when it is their turn to be interviewed. (Commercial breaks can be used as a time to re-arrange people.) Provide a prop microphone for the host. Other set props, such as a plant, table, rug or lamp, are optional. A sign telling the name of the show may serve as a background.

The "audience" must also prepare for their role. The audience will be made up of any group members who are not involved in other roles at any one time. The audience must respond to what is said by the host and guests. Also, they can ask questions of the guests.

After the production discuss the experience with the participants. Pass the prop microphone around and let each person respond individually to questions like "What did you learn from doing the production?" or "What advice would you like to give to people who are searching for happiness?" Remind the students of the need to seek God in all decisions.

Conclude with a time of spontaneous prayer. Suggest a topic of prayer and then allow a time of silence so that each person can pray about that topic individually and silently. If desired, begin the prayer with a few general petitions or thanksgivings to God. Then proceed with the response, "Lord, hear our prayer." Lead the group in praying for some or all of the following things:

> We thank you for the things which we learned today.
> We pray for the many people who are hungry for happiness.
> Please help to satisfy the people who are hungry for happiness.
> Please help me look for happiness in the right places.
> Thank you for the happiness you provide.
> AMEN.

Setting the Example

THAT YEAR HE SUPPLIED THEM WITH FOOD IN EXCHANGE FOR ALL THEIR LIVESTOCK.

Genesis 47:17

LEARN

The story of Joseph in the book of Genesis shows how God reconciled a family by satisfying their spiritual and physical hungers. The Bible records many other examples of people who fed the hungry. Using a game format the participants will read about some of these biblical people and about the different methods they used. They will discover a way that they too can feed the hungry.

LOCATE

✎ Large paper grocery bags

✎ Packages, cans, and bags of food

✎ Copies of Resource 1B, "Bible Situation Cards" (one for each small group)

✎ Copies of Resource 1C, "Contemporary Situation Cards" (one for each small group)

✎ Bibles

✎ Tables

✎ Paper, two colors

✎ Scissors or paper cutter

ADVANCE PREPARATION

✎ Duplicate the "Bible Situation Cards" and the "Contemporary Situation Cards" on two different colors of paper. Cut the cards apart and stack each set in a different pile.

✎ Arrange to gather enough food to fill one large grocery bag per small group. Announce ahead of time that participants should bring one or two food items to donate.

✎ Set up one table for each group of four to eight participants.

LEAD

The game is designed for four to eight participants. Divide the participants into small groups and direct them to their own tables. Set a paper grocery bag, a bible for each person, both sets of game cards, and a variety of cans, boxes, and bags of food on each table.

Read Genesis 47:13–17. Explain that this story is an example of what someone did to help hungry people. Tell the participants that they will play a game that will help them to discover other examples of people in the Bible who fed the hungry. Also, they will decide what people today can do to help feed the hungry.

The object of the game is to fill the grocery bag with food. This is accomplished by taking turns and working cooperatively to answer questions. Each time a question is answered a food package is placed in the bag. Everyone wins when the bag is filled!

Players alternate each turn choosing a card from both piles. Explain that the "Bible Situation Cards" describe scripture examples of people meeting the needs of the hungry. The "Contemporary Situation Cards" relate the hunger issues to modern people and times. The player who picks the card attempts to answer the question first. If it is a Bible question the player can immediately answer or can use a bible to look up the clue verse given at the bottom of the card. A "Contemporary Situation Card" may have several possible answers. The player can name all those he or she can think of. In either case, after one player has had an opportunity to answer, other players can add ideas or suggestions. The goal is to share as much information as possible. Encourage the participants to listen to each other and to speak clearly so that others can learn from their responses.

Make the point that everyone wins when people share what they have with others. Decide as a group what to do with the bag(s) of food. After the decision is made, close the session with a prayer. Stand around the food and pray for those who will receive it.

Bible Situation Cards (Answers):

1. Samaritan; 2. flour, oil; 3. Joseph; 4. 153; 5. Moses; 6. Ruth; 7. five thousand; 8. angel; 9. widows; 10. remembrance.

Recognizing the Hungry

IF YOU OFFER YOUR FOOD TO THE HUNGRY AND SATISFY THE NEEDS OF THE AFFLICTED, THEN YOUR LIGHT SHALL RISE IN THE DARKNESS AND YOUR GLOOM BE LIKE THE NOONDAY.

Isaiah 58:10

LEARN

Dance was a popular form of worship in the early Christian church. Today, dance can be used in worship services in conjunction with scripture readings, songs, and prayers to raise the level of spiritual awareness about hunger issues. Used in education, dance can help children explore and experience a variety of themes and concepts. Anyone can participate in a dance activity. Inexperienced and trained dancers, regardless of age and ability, can share in creating movements and pieces that range from simple to elaborate, concrete to abstract. In this activity, the participants will combine movement with the message of the song, "When I Was Hungry," for a presentation in a worship, education, or outreach setting. The dance movements for each verse are adapted with permission from *Liturgical Dance*.[1]

LOCATE

✎ Copies of Resource 1D, the music to "When I Was Hungry"[2]

✎ Instruments for musical accompaniment (optional)

✎ Hats or costume pieces

LEAD

Begin by dividing the participants into two groups labeled "haves" and "have-nots." The "have-nots" should wear bib overalls, sweatshirts, or caps. The "haves" should wear formal or business attire to identify them with the rich and powerful class. Ask the two groups to move to separate sides of the room. This can help to highlight the physical and cultural distance between the groups. As the song is sung each verse is enacted by the following movements:

Verse One Movements

Through writhing and twisting motions the "have-nots" show the intense suffering of hunger and thirst. Clenched fists are brought to the center of the body and turned one against the other. Movements to shield and conceal the body show the indignity of nakedness. Simultaneously the "haves" mingle with each other, oblivious to the human suffering near them. At the end of the verse, each "have-not" reaches out, hands open to the "haves" who busy themselves as if checking their watches.

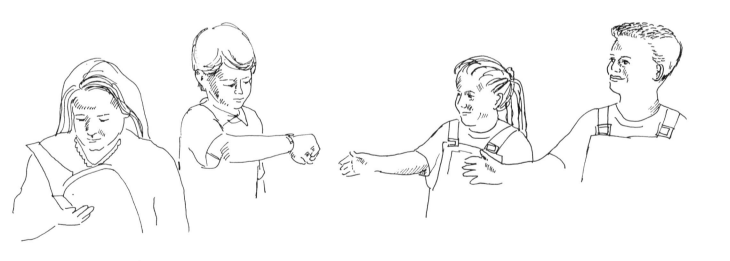

Verse Two Movements

The "have-nots" repeat their previous movement but remain fixed in one spot. The "haves" stroll through the group, taking casual notice, but remaining unimpressed by what they see. Toward the end of the verse, the "have-nots" kneel in a tight circle with their backs to one another as the "haves" stroll back to their original position.

Verse Three Movements

The "have-nots" join hands and rhythmically raise their heads and torsos in a wailing motion. The "haves" line up with their backs to the "have-nots," arms linked, and appear interested only in each other. The "have-nots" end the verse, weary of begging, with heads bowed and arms limp at their sides.

Verse Four Movements

The "haves" turn around to face the "have nots," but stay in their line, almost shoulder to shoulder but no longer connected. One person from the "have-nots" rises and approaches the first "have," placing cupped hands in the hands of the "haves." This movement symbolizes hunger. The first "have-not" promptly is pushed away and reels around to face the next "have," with the same results. Each "have" is confronted individually with the hand gesture but turns it away. As the "have-not" leaves the last "have" and twirls to a place in front of and a few feet away from him or her, the "have-not" stops and assumes the hunger pose.

A second "have-not" rises and approaches the aligned "haves." This time the gesture of confrontation represents weariness. The "have-not" attempts to rest his or her head on the shoulder of the "have" but is shrugged off by each in turn. Ultimately the second "have-not" lands with his or her head on the shoulder of the first "have-not." The "have-not" then assumes the weariness pose.

A third "have-not" then rises and approaches the "haves." The "have-not" holds his or her face as if crying and seeks comfort from each "have." The "have-not" is pushed away in the same manner as the others. The "have-not" ends up leaning against the first and second "have-nots" in the crying pose. They then, as one body, shuffle slowly a few feet further away from the "haves" line.

Verse Five Movements

A fourth "have-not" rises as the verse begins and approaches the first "have" with the hunger gesture, the next with the weariness gesture, and the last with the crying gesture. The "have-not" is brushed aside as the others were. As the "have-not" leaves the line, he or she stops momentarily between the "haves" and the huddled "have-nots." Then, while the lyric "We would have run to your side" is sung, the "haves" move in unison with arms outstretched to touch the solitary "have-not" as if they all suddenly realize that this last person was Jesus. Just as they reach the fourth "have-not," she or he moves away from them to join the other "have-nots."

Verse Six Movements

The supplication theme of verse three is repeated here. This time the "have-nots" stand in a cluster facing the audience with their backs to the "haves." They lift their arms and heads upward slowly, only to drop them back down, bodies bent to the floor. The "haves" remain in their places searching, looking past the "have-nots" for the vanished Christ. The "have-nots" rise again, and turn as they do so to face the "haves." At that moment, the "haves" sharply turn around, link arms, and walk away slowly. They end up in their original position mingling one with another. The "have-nots" also move back to their original position.

Verse Seven Movements

The dance for this verse is exactly like the dance of verse one. The "have-nots" hold their final position, reaching to the "haves" with open hands. The "haves" stroll casually off the stage, having left everything just as it was.

During the preparation time and following the presentation of "When I Was Hungry," be sure to process the message and the meaning of the words and movements with the participants. As an additional activity, re-read Matthew 25:35–45 and use a positive approach to interpret the scripture passage and the verses of the song. Re-write each verse, for example:

When I was hungry
You gave me something to eat.
When I was naked
You found shoes for my feet.
When I was thirsty
You gave me some of your wine.
I needed your hand, and you
shared your time.

Remind the participants that they will be both blessed and a blessing through helping others in Jesus' name.

---

1 Cornerstone Community of Stanton, VA. *Liturgical Dance*. Washington, DC: Bread for the World, 1981. Adapted with permission
2 Dowell, Joe. "When I Was Hungry." Washington, DC: Bread for the World. Used by permission.

Caring Through Prayer

"LORD, YOU KNOW EVERYTHING; YOU KNOW THAT I LOVE YOU."

John 21:17

LEARN

Peter wanted to serve Jesus. Jesus instructed Peter: "Feed my lambs. Tend my sheep." There are many hurting, lonely people who feel that no one cares for them. They hunger for love and affection. Through this activity the children will identify some of these people's needs and respond to them with prayer.

LOCATE

✎ Basket

✎ Scissors

✎ Crayons

✎ Pencils

✎ Four bibles

✎ Copies of Resource 1E, "Figure Patterns"

✎ Marker

ADVANCE PREPARATION

✎ Cut out and separate the people and bread figures on Resource 1E.

LEAD

Welcome the participants. Arrange chairs in a circle or sit with the group on the floor. Ask each person to share one interesting thing that has happened to them during the day. Show concern for and interest in the things which are shared.

After this time of casual conversation, assign four people to read the passage from John 21:1-18. Divide the reading among these parts:

◇ Narrator

◇ Jesus

◇ John ("the disciple whom Jesus loved")

◇ Peter

Present some background on the passage before reading it. This incident is set after Jesus' death and resurrection. The disciples have returned to their previous occupation, fishing, because they are not sure what else to do now that Jesus is no longer with them. Peter is the central character of this story. Just a few chapters before it was reported that Peter denied knowing Jesus three times. This appearance by Jesus in John 21 is described as the third time that Jesus revealed himself to his disciples after the resurrection.

Have the assigned participants read the story in parts. Then ask a volunteer to share a synopsis of the story line. Have the participants imagine more of what took place in the story. Ask: "How might the disciples have felt about Jesus' advice concerning fishing? What must the disciples have thought after they caught so many fish? What would it be like to share a meal with Jesus? How do you think Peter felt when he saw Jesus again? Why do you think Jesus asked Peter the same question three times? What do you think Jesus meant when he told Peter to feed his sheep?"

This story speaks of more than physical hunger. Peter's hunger was for Jesus' love and acceptance. Peter needed to be forgiven by Jesus. Jesus knew what Peter needed and was willing to feed him. Point out that there are many people who feel like Peter. They are hungry in many different ways. Some of them are *lonely, sad, rejected, abused, scared, guilty, angry, hurt,* or *unloved.* Distribute the people figures. Have the participants write these words on their figures. Allow the group to suggest other words to describe spiritual hunger. These can be added to the figures as well.

Next distribute the cutouts of the loaves of bread. Discuss what solutions are needed to feed the hungers listed on the people figures. For example, someone who is lonely needs a friend to listen to him or her. Someone who is guilty needs forgiveness. These solutions should be written on the bread loaf cutouts. After solutions for each hunger are written, the cutouts can be placed in a bread basket and set in the middle of the group.

When the basket is full, pass it around the circle and ask each person to take one piece of bread (it doesn't have to be his or her own). While holding the bread, the person is to pray for one way of feeding the hungry. Allow a time of silence after each person's prayer. Continue around the circle until everyone has addressed one hunger with a solution.

Sharing Your Resources

"NO ONE HAS GREATER LOVE THAN THIS, TO LAY DOWN ONE'S LIFE FOR ONE'S FRIENDS."

John 15:13

LEARN

The Japanese folktale *The Rabbit in the Moon*[1] will help the participants to discover the meaning of "laying down one's life for a friend." Through a dramatic re-enactment of the story they will learn that each person can use his or her own unique gifts to help those who are hungry.

LOCATE

- Brown paper grocery bags
- Plastic trash bags
- Medium rubber bands, two for each participant
- Staplers
- Markers
- Construction paper (8 1/2" X 11")
- Glue
- Scissors
- Yarn
- Resource 1F, "The Rabbit in the Moon" script
- Props (artificial banana, grapes, pear, orange, apple, seaweed, sticks) placed around the room
- Two Chairs

LEAD

Introduce the theme and present this summary of *The Rabbit in the Moon* to the group. Say:

The Rabbit in the Moon is the tale of an old man who lives on the moon. One day the old man decides to go to earth to locate the kindest animal in the forest. Disguised as a beggar, the man asks a variety of animals for food. Each animal brings the man something to eat. Although the rabbit too searches for food to share, he is sad because he does not find anything to present to the man. So, instead of food, he offers the man sticks, and tells him to use them to build a bonfire. Rabbit meat, he says, is very delicious. The old man realizes that because the rabbit is willing to offer the gift of himself, he is the kindest animal in the forest.

Assign or allow the participants to choose roles from the story to enact. The main characters are the old man and the rabbit. Depending on the number of participants, additional animals may be incorporated into the script or several children may construct the same type of animal.

Demonstrate the procedure for making "body puppets" that are actually worn by the children. Start with a full size brown paper grocery bag. The bottom flap becomes the puppet's head, and the rest of the bag forms the body. Have the participants draw or glue bits of construction paper on the flap to depict the face of their animal.

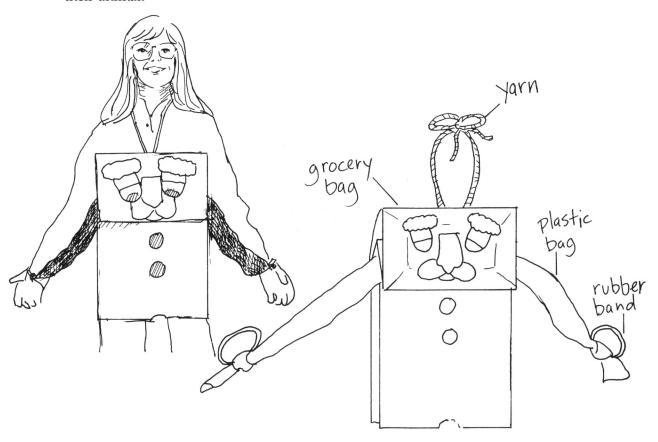

A neck strap is made by stapling a 30" X 2" piece of yarn to the middle of the top of the bag. For arms, cut two 18" X 2" strips of plastic bag. Tie a rubber band to the end of each piece of plastic. Staple the other end of each arm strip to the paper bag, just below the flap.

After the costumes are made, gather the group in a circle. Explain that the story will be presented in a participatory manner. Choose one person to guide the telling of the folktale as narrator. Give the narrator and the other characters a copy of the script (additional characters' lines can be written on the script). The narrator should read the lines slowly, giving the characters ample time to act out their parts. When the narrator mentions a particular animal, that serves as a cue for that character to get ready to participate in the story. Scatter the food props around the room. Tell the group that they are to look for them at the appropriate point in the play.

At the conclusion of the puppet show, invite the participants to share their reactions to the story. Ask: "How were all of the animals generous? Why was the rabbit kindest of all? What are some ways you can use your own talents and gifts to help feed the hungry?" Allow time for brainstorming. Then, if time permits, develop some of the responses to the third question into specific courses of action. Look for ways the participants can use their time, talents, and possessions to help to feed the hungry.

---

1 Pratt, David and Elsa Kula. *Magic Animals of Japan.* Berkeley, CA: Parnassus Press, 1967.

Multiplying the Food

"THERE IS A BOY HERE WHO HAS FIVE BARLEY LOAVES AND TWO FISH. BUT WHAT ARE THEY AMONG SO MANY PEOPLE?"

John 6:9

LEARN

The story of Jesus' multiplication of the fish and loaves will help the participants to discover that with God's power, every effort that they make to feed the hungry will be multiplied. With God's help, a little can turn into a lot! Use this rhythm story as a fun way of sharing this important truth.

LOCATE

✎ Copies of Resource 1G, "Multiplying the Food Rhythm Story"

Introduce the theme by reading John 6:1-14. Distribute Resource 1G, "Multiplying the Food Rhythm Story" to each participant. Choose five leaders or divide the participants into five small groups to chant assigned verses. Or, to use as an echo story, the leader or small group for each verse chants a line and the rest of the participants repeat or echo it back. When using the echo technique, first establish a clapping rhythm to accompany the chanting of the lines. A slap on the knees and a clap of the hands works well.

To extend the activity, have the participants brainstorm a list of things they could do to share food with hungry people. Then choose one idea from the list to develop. Instruct the participants to write a four-line verse (in the same style as the chant) about their way of sharing food. Recite together the additional verses and follow each with the refrain.

Remembering the Hungry

"GIVE US THIS DAY OUR DAILY BREAD."

Matthew 6:11

LEARN

In the Lord's Prayer we pray for the gift of daily bread, the daily subsistence necessary to live. In the parable of the last judgment, Jesus told of the importance of caring for those in need of food: "I was hungry and you fed me." In a society where food is plentiful for the majority, how easy it is to forget about those who do not receive an adequate share. During this art activity the participants will create a wooden spoon with a reminder of the hungry written on it that can be hung in the eating area of their homes. This project will help them to remember the hungry and to make good choices about their own eating.

LOCATE

- Wooden cooking spoons
- Thin satin ribbon or paper raffia
- Acrylic folk paint, several colors
- Paint brushes
- Paint containers
- White fine point paint marker
- Small dried or silk flowers (optional)

- Eye screws
- Scissors
- Posterboard
- Marker
- Protective materials for work surfaces
- Smocks
- Craft sample

ADVANCE PREPARATION

- Position the eye screws into the ends of the spoons.
- Prepare a sign which reads, "I was hungry and you fed me."

LEAD

Many people do not have the bread, or daily food, which they need in order to survive. It is important that those who do have enough food remember to pray daily for those who do not. Tell the group that they will be making a decorative spoon which will be a reminder to pray for, and to act on behalf of, the hungry.

The first step of this project is to have the participants paint the wooden spoon one basic color. Acrylic paints of different colors should be placed in containers so that they can be shared by several people. Each container should have its own brush. Make sure the participants wear smocks or other protective clothing while painting. Also, tell the participants not to apply an excessive amount of paint to the spoons or they will take a very long time to dry.

While the painted spoons are drying, have the participants meet in a circle on the floor. Use a sample spoon craft as a prop for a game. Say: "This spoon reminds me to pray for the homeless people who eat at the local soup kitchen." Then pass the spoon to the player on the right. That person repeats the phrase, "This spoon reminds me..." and finishes the sentence with an idea of his or her own. Some examples are:

"...to be very thankful for the food I have."

"...to volunteer at the food pantry."

"...to eat things that are good for me."

"...to not waste the food I am blessed to have."

Continue the game for as long as the participants have new contributions to make.

When the spoons are dry, move them to a table where decorating supplies are available. Have each student make a simple bow from ribbon or paper raffia and attach it to the spoon handle. If dried or silk flowers are available, they can be tied to the spoon handle as well.

White paint marker should be used to write the words, "I was hungry and you fed me," on the bowl of the spoon. Some participants could work on this step while others are decorating, so that less paint markers will be needed.

When all the steps have been completed, meet again in a circle with each participant holding his or her spoon. Close the session in prayer, asking God to help remind each person to care about, to pray for, and to help the hungry whenever possible.

Sharing the Word

AND AT HIS GATE LAY A POOR MAN NAMED LAZARUS, COVERED WITH SORES, WHO LONGED TO SATISFY HIS HUNGER WITH WHAT FELL FROM THE RICH MAN'S TABLE.

Luke 16:20–21

LEARN

In the story of Lazarus and the uncaring rich man (Lk 16:19-31), a hungry beggar is turned away without being helped. The rich man felt satisfied and did not care about the discomfort of someone less fortunate. It is sometimes easy for people who have food to forget about those who do not have food. While some people enjoy plenty, others struggle with hunger and starvation. The large scale problem of world hunger will be examined in this activity.

LOCATE

- Bread, various types
- Knife
- Napkins
- Paper, various colors, textures, and shapes
- Scissors
- Pens or markers

- Chalkboard or butcher paper
- Chalk or thick marker
- World map
- Copies of Resource 1H, "Sharing Food in a Hungry World Litany"[1]

ADVANCE PREPARATION

- Cut the paper into the shape and size of a slice of bread

LEAD

Explain that bread, in various forms and flavors, is generally the main staple of people's diets in all areas of the world. For some people, bread may be the only thing they eat in a day. Acquaint the pupils with various types of bread that are commonly used on the seven continents of the world. These may include:

◇ North America–cornbread

◇ South and Central America–tortillas

◇ Europe–rye

◇ Asia–rice cakes

◇ Africa–chapitas

◇ Australia–wheat

◇ Antarctica–marbled

Invite the group to sample as many selections as you have been able to gather. Show the children the world map and tell them that they will be learning more about the distribution of people and food in the world. Write these facts on the chalkboard or butcher paper detailing the percentage of the world's population living on each major continent:

◇ Africa–12%

◇ Asia–58%

◇ Europe–16%

◇ North America–6%

◇ South America–8%

Divide the participants into five groups approximating as closely as possible these percentages. For example, in a group of twenty-five participants, the Asia group might have fourteen members, Europe four, Africa three, and North and South America each two.

Hold up an uncut loaf of bread and explain that it represents all the food that will be eaten in the world in one day. Then divide the loaf according to the percentages of food consumed on the five major continents. Write these figures where all can see:

◇ Africa–8%

◇ Asia–23%

◇ Europe–36%

◇ North America–22%

◇ South America–11%

Give the pieces of bread to one person in each group.

Distribute copies of Resource 1H, "Sharing Food in a Hungry World Litany." Choose a leader and have the participants read it together, with each continent group responding in turn.

At the conclusion of the litany, ask the groups to share their bread together. There are two options for this experience: (1) Make sure that each person in the class has an equal portion to eat, or (2) tell the participants to share only within their own group. This second option allows the students to experience first-hand the unequal distribution of the world's food supply.

Continue the activity by brainstorming with the group about ways to gain more effective use of the bread staple. Ideas may include buying bread at a surplus store, finding out what grocery stores and bakeries do with day-old bread, and using stale bread for crumbs or croutons rather than throwing it away.

Pass out the papers which have been cut into the shapes of bread slices. Provide pens or markers and ask each child to write or draw a way in which he or she will commit to using bread more carefully and creatively so that all people of the world may have more to eat.

---

1 Church World Service Office on Global Education (Tom Hampson, Sandi McFadden, Phyllis Vos Wezeman, and Loretta Whalen). *Make a World of Difference: Creative Activities for Global Learning.* New York: Friendship Press, 1990. Adapted with permission.

TWO

I was thirsty

Overview

The Greek meaning for the word thirsty translates to "desperate." A thirst is a strong desire or craving that does not go away until it is satisfied. Physical thirst is satisfied when a person drinks liquid. However, there are other kinds of thirst besides physical thirst. Emotional and spiritual thirsts, for example, must be quenched in other ways.

The activities in this chapter will help to define what it means to thirst physically, emotionally, and spiritually. Suggestions for helping those who are thirsty will be explored. An appreciation for the important resource of water will be stressed and ways to conserve water will be emphasized. The simple act of giving a thirsty person something to drink is commended by Jesus in Matthew 25:35. Experiences in this chapter will help the participants explore ways to share both their literal and symbolic cups of water with others.

Thirsty for God

"BLESSED ARE THOSE WHO HUNGER AND THIRST FOR RIGHTEOUSNESS, FOR THEY WILL BE FILLED."

Matthew 5:6

LEARN

Though a difficult concept to understand, a person's thirst for God is as basic and important a need as the physical need for water. In this activity, the participants will create a sponge painting to help them link the need for water with their own spiritual need for God.

LOCATE

- Salted pretzels
- Napkins
- Two plants, one wilted and one healthy
- Watering can or cup and water
- Cardstock, folded to form a greeting card
- Scissors
- Tempera paints

- Sponges
- Table coverings
- Smocks
- Containers of water
- Flat containers for paint
- Paper towels
- Two large, clear glasses
- Paper
- Cold drinking water and cups
- Sink or catch basin

ADVANCE PREPARATION

- Wrap the two large glasses with plain paper. Write "God" on one and fill it with water. Fill one or more pitchers (depending on the number of participants) with ice water. If a sink is not available, place a catch basin nearby.

- Cover one or more tables with newspaper or recycled dry cleaning bags to use for painting. Set out smocks, wet paper towels, cardstock, and sponges cut into squares, circles, and other shapes.

 Pour various colors of paint into shallow containers.

 Make a sample card.

LEAD

As the participants arrive, offer them pretzels. Have them take a napkin full of pretzels to a suitable area for discussion. Do not give them anything to drink until later in the activity. As they eat the pretzels, talk about thirst. Ask: "When have you felt thirsty? What does it feel like to be thirsty?" Challenge the students to see how many ways the effects of thirst are witnessed in daily life. For example, people get dry mouths and ask for a drink, plants wilt, wood dries out, and land gets dusty and cracks.

Show the group one plant which has not been properly watered and one which has. Talk about the wilting plant's need for water. Choose someone from the group to water the plant. Some plants respond very quickly to watering and may even show a difference by the end of the activity.

Read Matthew 5:6 to the participants. Say: "Just as water is necessary for physical life, God is essential for spiritual life." Show the group a drinking glass that has been covered with plain paper. This glass should be empty, but do not make that obvious to the group. Ask: "What are some things besides God that people search for to make them feel happy?" Write their ideas (for example, money, clothing, power, fancy cars, and trim bodies) on the paper covering the glass. Then, ask: "How do these things permanently quench a person's thirst for happiness?" When it becomes obvious that they do not, tip the glass over and try to pour out its contents. Discuss the feeling of emptiness people find when they look for love, joy, and peace in the wrong places.

Next, hold up a drinking glass filled with water which has been covered with plain paper with the word "God" written on it. Ask: "How can God fill a person's thirst for happiness?" Record words on the glass to represent their ideas (for example, joy, love, strength, and truth). Then, ask: "How do these things permanently quench a person's thirst for happiness?" Pour out the contents of the glass into a sink or basin. Emphasize that God is always ready to quench a person's thirst for happiness? Produce the pitcher(s) of water. Say: "God has plenty of love and joy in reserve and will never run out!" Supply additional cups. Offer cups of cold water to the participants.

After this demonstration, show the group a dry sponge. Let each person touch it and feel how hard and unusable it is. Then put the sponge into water. Say: "If you absorb all that God offers, you too will always have what you need to feel happy. You, too, will have enough to share with others!" Allow everyone the chance to touch the wet sponge.

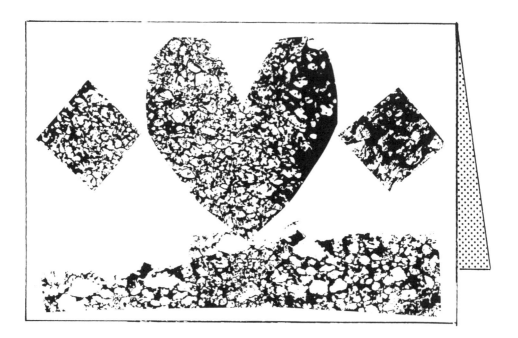

Direct the students to the painting table(s). Demonstrate how to dip the sponges in paint and to blot them on the paper to make a design. Instruct the participants to use sponges and paint to make a design on the front of the greeting. Allow each person to make as many cards as time allows.

When the cards are completed, set them aside to dry. Ask the participants to name people who have helped them to learn about God. Also ask: "Who are people you would like to share God's love with?" Encourage the students to write a note to one of these people on the inside of their cards. Arrange for the students to send their cards to the people they have named.

End the session by offering a prayer of thanks for God, who satisfies all thirsts.

Appreciating Water

GOD CALLED THE DRY LAND EARTH, AND THE WATERS
THAT WERE GATHERED TOGETHER HE CALLED SEAS.

Genesis 1:10

LEARN

Water is a wonderful and necessary part of God's creation. Unfortunately, due to a wide variety of factors water is not always as available, plentiful, or usable in some areas as it is in others. Because of this, water is a gift that cannot be wasted or spoiled. In this art and writing activity, the participants will discover ways that water is misused. They will also gain a greater appreciation for the gift of water by learning of the scarcity of free-flowing, germ-free water in many areas of the world.

LOCATE

- Chalk (various colors to represent shades of water)
- Chalkboard or large sheet of mural paper
- Plain paper
- Scratch paper
- Pencils
- Pens or dark markers
- Masking tape

ADVANCE PREPARATION

- Tape mural paper to a wall or place it on a table or the floor (optional).

LEAD

Provide pieces of different colored chalk. Include shades associated with clean water (especially pastel colors like blues, greens, and yellows). Ask the participants to use the chalk to color a chalkboard or mural paper in the form of a large body of water. Make sure everyone has enough space and opportunity to contribute to the joint project.

When the mural is complete, gather everyone nearby and read Genesis 1:6–10. Distribute a sheet of white paper to each person. Tell the students to use the chalk to draw their own individual versions of the mural, filling the entire page with their impressions of water. Encourage the participants to experiment with different stroke textures; demonstrate, for example, dark dashes made with the point of the chalk and wide, flowing strokes done with the side of the chalk. Provide extra sheets of paper for students who work quickly or who would like to draw more than one picture. When the allotted time is up, have the participants set their pictures aside.

Next, return to the large mural. Brainstorm with the participants some of the ways that people waste water. Using dark colored chalk, write or have each person write his or her idea on the mural. At the top of the mural, write a caption or statement developed by the group that ties the ideas together. Challenge the students to think of one or two ways they personally waste water and to make a commitment to work at changing their behavior. Have them write these ideas at the top of the individual water drawings. If the mural is movable, it can be displayed in an open hallway or bulletin board to help remind others of the importance of water.

Provide scratch paper and pencils to the participants. Ask them to write five words that describe water and a summary statement about water at the bottom of the list. For example:

> Refreshing
> Cool
> Smooth
> Bubbling
> Flowing
> Water makes me new again.

The participants have now created water poems. To make the assignment more challenging, have the participants add a descriptive phrase after each word. Then, the sample poem might read like this:

> Refreshing pouring over me,
> Cool against my hands and face,
> Smooth as I run my hands over it,
> Bubbling as it runs over me,
> Flowing all around me,
> Water makes me new again.

After the first drafts have been completed provide pens or markers and have the students write their poems on top of their individual chalk drawings. Then direct them to share their poems in one of the following ways:

1. They can sit together in a circle and show them to other group members.
2. The poems can be read aloud by the authors or one designated leader.
3. The drawings can be displayed on a bulletin board.
4. Older students can pass the drawings round robin style, taking some time to read each poem.
5. The drawings can be collected and bound in one folder and left on display for individual reading.

Conclude the activity by gathering the participants together for a few moments of quietness. Ask them to silently review their own poems, using them as a prayer of thanksgiving to God for the gift of water.

Quenching a Thirst

"I AM STANDING HERE BY THE SPRING OF WATER; LET THE YOUNG WOMAN WHO COMES OUT TO DRAW, TO WHOM I SHALL SAY, 'PLEASE GIVE ME A LITTLE WATER FROM YOUR JAR TO DRINK' . . ."

Genesis 24:43

LEARN

When Rebekah offered Isaac's servant a drink of water after his long journey, it was a sign of kindness and compassion. Soon after, according to the text in the book of Genesis, Isaac and Rebekah were married. Sharing the life-sustaining gift of water with others is an important element of Christian ministry. In this activity the participants will create an origami drinking cup and will participate in a clown skit that will help them to discover how they are called to minister in Jesus' name.

LOCATE

- ✎ 8" squares of freezer wrap
- ✎ Pens or pencils
- ✎ Hats, various styles (optional)
- ✎ Red stickers
- ✎ Water pitcher with water

LEAD

Introduce the activity by helping each participant make an origami drinking cup. *Origami* means "paper folding" in Japanese. This simple cup will be used in a skit utilizing the timeless, dramatic technique of clowning. It will also serve as a reminder of Jesus' instructions to minister to others in his name.

Give each person an 8" square of sturdy freezer wrap that is coated with wax on one side. Make sure that the participants place the waxed surface facing up. Then, instruct them in the following steps:

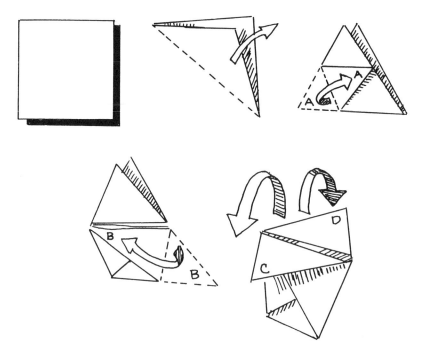

1. Fold the paper in half diagonally, to form a triangle.
2. Fold the left hand corner to the middle of the opposite side.
3. Fold the right hand corner to the middle of the opposite side.
4. Note the two layers of paper that form the triangle at the top of the cup. Fold one layer forward, and the other layer back. The cup is complete and ready to use as a drinking glass.

Gather the participants with their cups in a circle. Read aloud Genesis 24:43–46 about Abraham's servant's need for a drink of water. Tell the group that they will be preparing and presenting a skit, taking the roles of clowns, in which they will express the needs of thirsty people. Next, mention different kinds of people who have physical thirsts; for example, young children, teens, and older adults. Ask each participant to write a word describing one of these categories of people on one side of their cup. On the other side, have them write a word describing a place where their thirsty person could likely be found; for example, the word "teen-ager" might be matched with "athletic field" and "older adult" with "nursing home." Encourage as much variety as possible. Tell the participants that the people and places they have written on their cups describe the characters they will portray in the clown skit.

Clown costumes can easily be created by asking the children to change three things about their clothing. Suggest ideas like rolling up one pant leg, putting a shirt on backwards, and wearing shoes on the wrong feet. If hats are available, let each person choose one to wear. Place a red circle sticker on everyone's nose to signify the mark of the clown.

Explain the basic premise of the story: Two clowns, Care and Careless, set off on a journey. Each clown carries a container of water which holds just enough water to last for the duration of the trip. Along the way Care and Careless meet various clowns who are thirsty and in need of a drink of water. (Those who play the roles of thirsty clowns must communicate their need verbally or nonverbally to Care and Careless.) Care always shares from the limited supply, yet the water never runs out.

Careless does not share. Careless not only drinks the water, but also wastes it by spilling it all over the place.

Choose participants for the various roles. Position the thirsty clowns on a "path" in the room. Proceed with encounters between the thirsty clowns and Care and Careless. The skit concludes with Careless completely out of water. Care and the others must now decide what to do about Careless. Conduct a follow-up discussion in which the participants debate possible solutions to the problem. Accept all solutions, but remind the participants of their responsibility to share this vital gift of water with others.

Discovering Water Facts

WHEN THE POOR AND NEEDY SEEK WATER, AND THERE IS NONE, AND THEIR TONGUE IS PARCHED WITH THIRST, I THE LORD WILL ANSWER THEM, I THE GOD OF ISRAEL WILL NOT FORSAKE THEM.

Isaiah 41:17

LEARN

In the United States, most people turn on a faucet and treated, drinkable water flows out of it. In other parts of the world, water must be drawn and carried from a stream, well, or spring. In either case, water is a resource that must be guarded and cared for by everyone. Use the following game format to help the participants discover some important information about water.

LOCATE

- Bible
- Ten traditional water buckets
- Ten adhesive labels
- Water conservation items (see "Water Conservation" bucket in *Lead* section)
- Permanent markers
- Copy of Resource 2A, "Discovering Water Facts Game Cards"
- Copies of Resource 2B, "Discovering Water Facts Game Sheet" (optional)
- Pens, pencils, or markers
- Large poster paper or a white bedsheet that is ready to be discarded
- Dice
- Buttons to use as game markers
- Sidewalk chalk (optional)
- Paper

ADVANCE PREPARATION

- Label one bucket with each of the following categories:

  1. Water Conservation
  2. Water Cycle
  3. Water Facts
  4. Water Memories
  5. Water Pollution
  6. Water Scripture Stories/Verses
  7. Water Songs
  8. Water Uses
  9. Water Concerns
  10. Water Projects

✎ Prepare one large game board on a large piece of poster paper or an old white bed sheet. Or, to play the game outside, draw the game board on a sidewalk or parking lot with chalk. See Resource 2B for an example.

LEAD

Introduce the game by pointing out the ten buckets and ten themes that will be used. Explain that for each theme, players will either share a fact, offer an opinion, or answer a question. Suggested activities for each theme include:

Water Conservation

Players will name one method of conserving water. Place items like rubber washers, shower nozzles, laundry soap, a seed package of a plant that needs little water, and a small hand broom in the bucket. When a player lands on this space he or she chooses an item and either names a method of conserving water related to the item (for example, shower nozzle/take shorter showers, or hand broom/sweep rather than hose your sidewalk) or a method not related to the item.

Water Cycle

Players will answer true or false statements about the water cycle. Place five true/false statement cards in the bucket (see Resource 2A). When a player lands on this space, he or she draws one card and answers the question or asks for help from the other participants. *Answers:* (1) true; (2) false; (3) true; (4) true; (5) false.

Water Facts

Players will read a fact about water. Place five fact statement cards in the bucket (see Resource 2A). When a player lands on this space, he or she draws one card and reads the statement to the group.

Water Memories

Players will share a memory of an experience in which water was the focus. Place five memory cards in the bucket (see Resource 2A). When a player lands on this space, he or she draws one card and relates a personal memory or experience based on the suggestion.

Water Pollution

Players will select a correct answer to a multiple choice question on water pollution. Place five multiple choice questions related to water pollution in the bucket (see Resource 2A). When a player lands on this space, he or she draws one card and answers the question or asks for help from the other participants. *Answers:* (1) b; (2) c; (3) c; (4) a; (5) c.

Water Scripture Stories/Verses

Players will recite a scripture verse or share a scripture story related to water. Place five cards with scripture references for water-related stories in the bucket (see Resource 2A). Also, place one bible in the bucket. When the player lands on this space, he or she draws one card and either reads the assigned scripture passage from the Bible or paraphrases it in his or her own words.

Water Song

Players will guess the names of a song related to water. Place five cards with the names of songs with water references in their titles in the bucket (see Resource 2A). When the player lands on this space, her or she draws one card and tries to elicit the title from the other participants. This may be done through pantomime or by listing a space for each letter and then playing the game "Hangman."

Water Uses

Players will suggest a general or specific use for water. Place five cards with different general uses for water in the bucket (see Resource 2A). When the player lands on this space, he or she draws one card and gives a specific example for each general use (for example, surfing/recreation, or irrigation/farming) or suggests another general category (for example, "putting out fires").

Water Concerns

Players will answer a yes or no question on an important issue or concern involving water. Place five yes or no water concern questions in the bucket (see Resource 2A). When a player lands on this space, he or she draws one card and answers the question or asks for help from the other participants. *Answers:* (1) no; (2) yes; (3) yes; (4) yes; (5) yes.

Water Projects

Players will read information about a current water-related project or organization that is currently active in the world. Place five cards with information about a current water-related project or organization in the bucket (see Resource 2A). When a player lands on this space, he or she draws one card and reads the statement to the group.

Get ready to play the game! Have all the students participate. Use one large game board placed on the floor or wall. Choose one player to throw the die and move that number of spaces. The player then calls out the category and chooses one item or card from the bucket. If an answer is required the player may give it himself or herself or ask for help from the group. Continue the game until each person has at least one turn.

If the students are interested in playing the game at home, distribute copies of Resource 2B, "Discovering Water Facts Game Sheet." Suggest that the students share the activity with family and friends using questions and statements they research and develop on their own.

Refreshing Water Themes

THEY ARE LIKE TREES PLANTED BY STREAMS OF WATER, WHICH YIELD THEIR FRUIT IN ITS SEASON, AND THEIR LEAVES DO NOT WITHER. IN ALL THAT THEY DO, THEY PROSPER.

Psalm 1:3

LEARN

One of water's greatest qualities is as a refreshment. A glass of ice water on a hot day quenches thirst; a gentle rainfall revives wilting plants and cleanses well-worn buildings. Because of this unique quality of renewal, water is also used as a symbol of spiritual refreshment. The passage from the book of Psalms expresses the belief that those who depend on God—like trees planted by streams—are revitalized. Through the use of water, music, and other related symbols, this activity will help the participants understand the importance of physical, emotional, and spiritual renewal and refreshment.

LOCATE

- ✎ Objects associated with water's renewing quality, for example: (1) a clear glass or pitcher; (2) a wash cloth; (3) a bathing suit; (4) a sprinkling can; (5) a nozzle or hose; (6) a squirt gun; (7) a pet dish for water; (8) a toy boat; (9) a vase; (10) a record, cassette, or CD with water-related music themes.
- ✎ Record, cassette, or CD player
- ✎ Large shopping bags (one for each object)

ADVANCE PREPARATION

- ✎ Place one object related to water's refreshing quality in each large shopping bag.

LEAD

There are many objects that can be connected with water's important quality of renewal. Help the participants explore this concept by following the directions for this activity. First, randomly distribute the bags with water-related objects to various participants. (Do not distribute the bag with the record, cassette, or CD, however.) Call on the people with the bags one at a time to remove the object and show it to others. Lead a discussion on how each object can be used to renew or refresh someone or something. For example:

1. A **glass of water** can be given to someone who is thirsty.
2. A **wash cloth** can clean a dirty face.
3. A **bathing suit** can be used for a swim on a hot day.
4. A **sprinkling can** can be used for watering house plants.
5. A **nozzle or hose** can be used for watering an outdoor lawn or garden.
6. A **toy squirt gun** can be used for frolicking and fun.
7. A **pet dish** with water is a necessity for reviving a thirsty animal.
8. A **boat** can be used for travel or for taking a relaxing ride.
9. A **vase** is needed to keep flowers alive.

After discussing each item, produce the bag with the recording of water-themed music. Tell the group that it is a musical recording. Ask: "How can music renew and refresh you?" Point out that everyone needs to be renewed in body, mind, and spirit and that music is one method many people use to become revived and revitalized.

Invite the group to listen to different kinds of music with water-related titles, themes, and lyrics. If possible, play selections ranging from calypso to classical, rag to rock, and pop to polka.

After playing a variety of music ask the students how the music makes them feel. Ask: "What type of music calms and relaxes you? What type of music excites you?" Encourage a variety of responses.

Conclude the activity by offering spontaneous prayers thanking God for the ways in which the gift of water refreshes people physically, emotionally, and spiritually.

Praising God for Water

YOU WATER ITS FURROWS ABUNDANTLY, SETTLING ITS RIDGES, SOFTENING IT WITH SHOWERS, AND BLESSING ITS GROWTH.

Psalm 65:10

LEARN

Water is the most essential of all life-sustaining elements. A person needs one and one-half quarts of water a day on the average in order to survive. Although water is our most basic resource, it is, unfortunately, often the one most taken for granted. Through involvement in this prayer activity, participants will thank God for water and discover new ways to conserve and appreciate this important gift.

LOCATE

✎ Newsprint

✎ Markers

✎ Construction paper

✎ Scissors

✎ Alphabet stencil patterns (optional)

✎ Globe or world map

✎ Cut out block upper case letters of the alphabet from construction paper. As an option, you may wish to purchase precut stencils.

✎ Prepare three pieces of newsprint for the introductory activity, each large enough to display in the room. Write one of these words on each sheet: Morning, Afternoon, Evening. Hang the newsprint where all can see.

LEAD

Supply one marker to each participant. Have them write words or draw pictures on the appropriate newsprint of ways in which they use water at these times during the day. Allow time for the participants to explain and share what they write or draw.

Distribute one or more letters of the alphabet to each participant. (Make sure each person is holding consecutive letters; for example A-B-C or M-N.) Have the group display the letter(s) they received in front of them and form a circle in alphabetical order. Start this prayer with words such as "God, we thank you for every use of water." Then, beginning with the person holding the "A," direct each person, in turn, to name a use of water that starts with the letter(s) they are holding. Encourage the group to help each other come up with ideas. Continue around the circle until everyone has contributed an idea. Suggested words include:

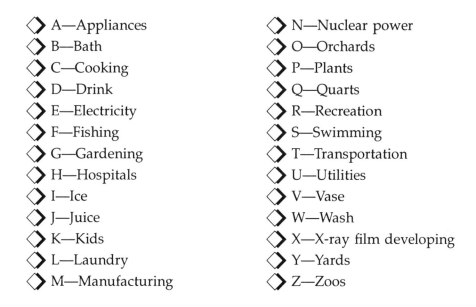

◇ A—Appliances
◇ B—Bath
◇ C—Cooking
◇ D—Drink
◇ E—Electricity
◇ F—Fishing
◇ G—Gardening
◇ H—Hospitals
◇ I—Ice
◇ J—Juice
◇ K—Kids
◇ L—Laundry
◇ M—Manufacturing
◇ N—Nuclear power
◇ O—Orchards
◇ P—Plants
◇ Q—Quarts
◇ R—Recreation
◇ S—Swimming
◇ T—Transportation
◇ U—Utilities
◇ V—Vase
◇ W—Wash
◇ X—X-ray film developing
◇ Y—Yards
◇ Z—Zoos

Go through the alphabet more than once, if possible. Conclude the prayer by having everyone sing or say "Amen."

Explain the need for water conservation. The participants will use their letters to help them think of ways that water can be conserved. If you wish, have the group exchange letters and then reform the circle in alphabetical order. Hold up a globe or a map. Ask the students to guess the percentage of water that covers the earth (70 percent). Point out that 97 percent of the earth's water is salt water. Another two percent is trapped in glaciers and ice caps. Only one percent of the earth's water is contained in lakes, rivers, and underground wells. Although ocean water is desalinated in some places, there is not as much usable drinking water in the world as one might imagine. Also, great amounts of water are wasted. Therefore, it is important to conserve water so there will be enough for everyone in the world. Repeat the same process as before, this time taking turns naming conservation-related words beginning with each letter. Conservation words include:

- A—Agriculture (crop management)
- B—Broom (sweep instead of hosing off sidewalks)
- C—Compost
- D—Displacement devices
- E—Energy
- F—Full loads in machines
- G—Grass (cut less often)
- H—Hose
- I—Instruct
- J—Justice issues
- K—Knowledge
- L—Leaks (repair)
- M—Mulch
- N—Nozzles
- O—Organizations
- P—Presoak
- Q—Question
- R—Repair
- S—Short shower
- T—Trees
- U—Used water (recycled for watering gardens)
- V—Views (exchange them with others)
- W—Water saving appliances
- X—X-tra effort!
- Y—Yards (landscape with plants needing little water)
- Z—Zoning

After the group has explored conservation options, lead them in a prayer. Ask God to help each person do his or her part to conserve water.

Exploring Pollution Problems

WHEN THEY CAME TO MARAH, THEY COULD NOT DRINK THE WATER OF MARAH BECAUSE IT WAS BITTER.

Exodus 15:23

LEARN

It is estimated that by the start of the twenty-first century as much as one-fourth of the world's reliable water supply could be unsafe for human consumption because of pollution. In this activity, participants will learn about water pollution problems and share possible solutions.

LOCATE

- Paint can
- Motor oil can or advertisement
- Lawn fertilizer wrapper or advertisement
- Fishing line
- Photo of underground storage tanks
- Trash (discarded wrappers)
- Insecticide box, can, or advertisement
- Oven cleaner box or advertisement
- Hypodermic needle case or plastic syringe
- Tray
- Paper
- Pencils or pens

ADVANCE PREPARATION

- Prepare a tray containing actual items or photos to represent the following items for this acronym:

P—Paint
O—Oil (motor)
L—Lawn fertilizer
L—Line (fishing)
U—Underground storage tanks
T—Trash (discarded wrappers)
I—Insecticide
O—Oven cleaner
N—Needle (case or plastic syringe)

LEAD

Give a brief overview of the current problem of water pollution. Say:

Water pollution is a serious threat to the world's supply of consumable water. Most water comes from one of two sources: surface waters such as lakes and rivers, or deep underground wells or aquifers. Both of these sources are threatened. Almost everything that is put on the ground ends up in the water. For example, when rain or irrigation water washes across the land surface, things like salts used to de-ice highways, motor oil from streets, and hazardous chemicals stored in municipal landfills are washed into rivers and streams or soak into the groundwater. The resulting pollution is likely to cause many problems to humans and marine life including disease, birth defects, and death.

Distribute paper and a pencil to each person. Then read Exodus 15:23 to the group. Say:

> You will be shown a tray containing nine examples of objects related to the theme of this Bible verse. Some of the examples will be actual objects, others will be photos of the objects. You will have one minute to study the tray. Try to memorize all nine items. You will have another minute to write as many items as you can remember on the sheet of paper.

After allowing enough time for both steps, tell the students that the first letters of the nine words should form an acronym, pollution. Have the students work with a partner or in a small group to check their answers and to discuss how each item contributes to the problem of water pollution. Ask the participants to name additional sources of water pollution.

As an extension to this activity, you may wish to have the students report on one or more of the major causes of water pollution and share their findings with the group. You can either provide research materials or have the students prepare their report at the library from materials they gather on their own.

Living Water

"THE WATER THAT I WILL GIVE WILL BECOME IN THEM A SPRING OF WATER GUSHING UP TO ETERNAL LIFE."

John 4:14

LEARN

In a conversation with a Samaritan woman, Jesus offered the gift of spiritual water; water which would always be readily available and which would never run out. Spiritual water is the water of life, the water that quenches all earthly worries and anxieties. In this activity, the participants will make individual booklets to help them to experience the reality of this life-giving truth.

LOCATE

- Personal photos or magazine photos of water
- Scissors
- Glue sticks
- Markers
- Bibles

- Bible Concordance (optional)
- Copies of Resource 2C, "Scripture Verse Options" (optional)
- Chalk, paint, or colored pencils and paper
- Hole punch and brads, yarn, ribbon, or rings

LEAD

Read John 4:13–15 to the group. Discuss the description of Jesus as living water. Ask: "How is Jesus like water? How is Jesus necessary for life? What difference does Jesus make in your life?" Make sure the students understand that as their bodies cannot live without physical water, their spirits cannot truly live without the living water which Jesus provides.

Invite the group to develop a booklet that illustrates this theme. To do this, first have the students use a bible concordance to help them locate scripture verses that offer other descriptions of living water. Or, they may use the list provided (see Resource 2C, "Scripture Verse Options"). The students should look up and read these passages from the Bible to determine the ones they would like to illustrate.

Next, assign the participants to choose photos or create their own pictures which illustrate the scripture verses. You may wish to supply a large selection of old magazines, calendars, and travel brochures that can be gleaned of appropriate material. Also, the participants can bring in personal photos that include not only water, but examples of the abundant life that Jesus promised. Encourage artistic students to use various art mediums (for example, paint, chalk, or colored pencils) to create various water scenes like lakes, streams, or oceans. In either case, mount the photos or illustrations on the same size of colored construction paper so that the pages of the booklet will be uniform.

When the illustrations are mounted choose several students to print a scripture verse on each page. Brainstorm a title for the booklet with the students and have them make a title page. Punch three uniform holes in the pages. Bind the pages together using brads, yarn, ribbon, or rings.

Display the book so that everyone can see it. Arrange to have the booklet placed on display at an event where the entire church community might appreciate the effort as well as Jesus' presence in their lives as living water. Or, the booklet can be displayed as part of a presentation conducted by your group (perhaps directed to younger children). The following questions may be included in the presentation: (1) What does Jesus' living water mean to you? (2) How do you experience the living water of Jesus? How do you seek to share it with others?

Flowing with Justice

BUT LET JUSTICE ROLL DOWN LIKE WATERS, AND
RIGHTEOUSNESS LIKE AN EVERFLOWING STREAM.

Amos 5:24

LEARN

The quotation from the prophet Amos is one of many powerful statements about justice from the Hebrew scriptures. Amos uses the image of ever-flowing water to describe the common human need for righteousness and fair treatment. This activity will help the participants weave definitions, scripture verses, and personal statements about justice together to form a litany for their common recitation.

L O C A T E

- ✎ Paper
- ✎ Pencils
- ✎ Chalkboard or newsprint and masking tape (optional)

- ✎ Chalk (optional)
- ✎ Markers (optional)
- ✎ Overhead projector, transparencies, and markers (optional)

L E A D

Divide the participants into two groups. Say: "Everyone with a birthday between January and June sit together on one side of the room and everyone with a birthday from July to December sit on the other side." After the groups are formed name one the "justice" team and the other the "righteousness" team. Read the passage from Amos 5:24. Have the groups chant the passage in two parts. The justice team chants, "Let justice roll down like waters." The righteousness team answers, "And righteousness like an everflowing stream." Have the teams repeat the phrases back and forth several times. End the exercise by having both groups clap their hands rhythmically in unison.

Next, provide working space, paper, and pencils for each group. Ask the justice team to brainstorm definitions and examples of the word justice and the righteousness team to do the same for the word righteousness. Then have each group pool their responses together and write five statements about the meaning of their assigned word. For example, the justice team will write, "Justice is . . ." and complete five sentences. The righteousness team will write, "Righteousness is . . ." and complete five sentences.

After the groups have compiled five statements, the statements will be combined with the Amos 5:24 verse to form a litany. The litany pattern goes like this:

Justice:	Let justice roll down like waters.
Righteousness:	And righteousness like an everflowing stream.
Justice:	Justice is . . . (Statement 1)
	Let justice roll down like waters.
Righteousness:	And righteousness like an everflowing stream.
	Righteousness is . . . (Statement 1)
Justice:	Let justice roll down like waters.
Righteousness:	And righteousness like an everflowing stream.
Justice:	Justice is . . . (Statement 2)
	Let justice roll down like waters.

(The pattern continues until each team's five statements have been recited. The litany concludes with the Amos 5:24 chant being repeated twice.)

Have both groups work together to print the litany on newsprint, a chalkboard, or on an overhead transparency. Use various colors of markers or chalk, if possible.

The litany should be recited together by both groups, with each group reading its statements in turn. You may assign each line to be read by the entire justice or righteousness group, or to individuals from each group. The refrain from Amos should be spoken in unison.

This activity could be extended by having the students illustrate the justice and righteousness statements and collecting their art work into one portfolio. The portfolio can be displayed so that others in the congregation might become more aware of this issue and the students' efforts.

Filling a Cup in Jesus' Name

FOR TRULY I TELL YOU, WHOEVER GIVES YOU A CUP OF WATER TO DRINK BECAUSE YOU BEAR THE NAME OF CHRIST WILL BY NO MEANS LOSE THE REWARD.

Mark 9:41

LEARN

A reward is promised to those who bring drink to the thirsty. Jesus' words are a reminder that we minister to others and are ministered to because we are part of the same Christian family. When we bring a drink to the thirsty we quench a physical need. When we bring an expression of love we quench a spiritual need. In this activity the participants will shape a cup out of clay to remind them of the many ways to serve Jesus by serving others.

LOCATE

✎ Clay cup

✎ Self-drying clay, cut into individual pieces for each participant

✎ Paper towels

✎ Wet cloths

✎ Newspapers

✎ Blunt tools and instruments (for example, craft sticks, toothpicks, flatware, and small tools)

LEAD

Propose this question to the group: "Who are people you know who are in need of a drink of water?" Pass a clay cup around the circle of participants and ask each person to tell a way in which it could be used to bring a drink of water to someone in Jesus' name. Each participant should begin with the phrase, "In Jesus' name I could use this cup to . . ." Possible responses are "to give my little sister a drink, since she can't reach the faucet," or, "to share some water with a friend who just finished a race." Make sure that everyone has the chance to share at least one idea.

Next, prepare the area for an art project. Provide each participant with newspaper and wet cloths for his or her work space. Give each person a piece of clay. Say:

> Get a feel for the clay by molding it in your hands. Soften it by working it into different shapes in your palms and fingers. Make the clay pliable but don't try to make an object. Rather, discover what you can do with the clay by changing it in many different ways.

After they have worked with the clay for a little while, ask the participants to form it into something that symbolizes an abundance of water. Tell them to use their imaginations to choose what shapes they will make. One person might form many drops of water, another might flatten the clay in the shape of a lake. Allow the participants the chance to explain their symbols to others. Then ask them to form the clay into a symbol for a lack of water. This could be a concrete symbol like wilting flowers, or something that represents a feeling like a person's expression of despair.

Finally, read Mark 9:41 to the participants. Ask them to use their clay to shape a drinking cup. Encourage them to be creative and to design their cups in a unique way. Provide simple, blunt tools for them to use to make designs, etch symbols, or to further shape the surface of the clay. When complete, allow more time for the participants to share their work with each other and to explain any special features or meanings of their cups.

Ask the group members to hold their finished cups in their hands. Go around the circle, allowing each person to complete the prayer sentence, "Thank you, God, that I received water in your name when . . ." After each person has said a prayer of thanks, continue with prayers of petition. Have them complete the sentence, "Help me to offer a cup of water in your name by . . ."

Before the participants leave, instruct them to wrap their cups in damp paper towels in order to transport them home. At home, the cups should be set out until dry. Inform the participants that since the clay has not been treated properly, the cups are not safe for drinking.

THREE

I was a stranger

Overview

Unfortunately, *stranger* has become a negative word in our culture. It calls to mind someone who may be dangerous. Our immediate response to a stranger is caution. Parents rightfully protect their children by giving them warnings of this type.

Sojourner is a term that more closely describes the intended meaning of stranger in the Bible. A sojourner is one who travels through or lives in a place which is uncomfortable or strange to him or her. This person does not have any roots in the area, any relatives or friends nearby. Sojourners are dependent on the hospitality of those people they meet. In some ways all Christians are strangers or sojourners. Today, popular culture is becoming increasingly alien to Christian lifestyles and values. The activities in this chapter will explore more of the characteristics of this type of alienation.

The Bible provides a model for how sojourners should be treated. The wandering Israelites of the Old Testament were in fact sojourners who moved through the desert or settled among foreign people, depending only on the hospitality of others in God's name to survive. In the New Testament, Jesus often welcomed or was welcomed by strangers. The New Testament letters (1 Timothy 3:2 and Titus 1:8) list hospitality as one of the primary qualities which church leaders should display.

The ten activities in this chapter offer a variety of suggestions and techniques for exploring many aspects of the theme, "I was a stranger."

Living Hospitality

BE HOSPITABLE TO ONE ANOTHER WITHOUT COMPLAINING. LIKE GOOD STEWARDS OF THE MANIFOLD GRACE OF GOD, SERVE ONE ANOTHER WITH WHATEVER GIFT EACH OF YOU HAS RECEIVED.

1 Peter 4:9–10

LEARN

Friends who accept the invitation to visit our homes should feel welcome there. What are some signs of welcome in your own home? In this activity the participants will make decorations to hang in their homes to express their family's open welcome to all who pass through their doorways.

LOCATE

- 3″ grapevine wreaths
- Wooden spoons or craft sticks
- Acrylic craft paint for wood
- Paint brushes
- Paint markers
- Colored 1 yd. X 1/4″ paper raffia ribbon
- Colored 4″ X 1/4″ paper raffia ribbon
- Colored 8″ X 1/4″ paper raffia ribbon
- Tacky glue
- Toothpicks
- Smocks
- Table covering(s)

ADVANCE PREPARATION

- Cover table(s) with newspaper or butcher paper to protect during painting.
- Precut the pieces of paper raffia ribbon for each participant.

LEAD

Ask the participants to share examples of things which make a home appear inviting. Examples might include open curtains, a shining light, or a shoveled sidewalk on a winter day. Also ask: "What are some signs of welcome in your own home?" You might wish to list the suggestions on the chalkboard or a piece of butcher paper.

Tell the participants that they will be making a sign of welcome that can be displayed in their homes. Distribute painting smocks and one 3" grapevine wreath to each person. Gather the group around a table(s). Paint brushes, paint containers with one color of acrylic paint, and paper raffia ribbon should be within the reach of each person for sharing. The color of the paper raffia ribbon should match or complement the paint color, since not much of either supply is needed.

Instruct the participants to paint the entire wooden spoon or craft stick and allow it to dry completely. When the sticks are dry, have each person write the word "Welcome" on his or her stick, using a complementary color of paint marker.

Help the participants make bows out of the paper raffia ribbon. Precut three pieces of paper raffia ribbon per participant (one 1 yard piece, one 8" piece, and one 4" piece). Demonstrate how to make a bow by folding the 1 yard piece as an accordion, back and forth in 3" sections. Hold the folded piece tightly in the middle and tie the 4" piece of raffia ribbon around its center, securing it with a double knot. Show the students how to glue the bow in place on the top or bottom of the wreath. (Use a craft stick or toothpick to spread the tacky glue liberally.) Loop the 8" piece of raffia through the center of the wreath and tie it in a knot. This piece can be used to hang the wreath.

The decoration is completed by gluing the painted "Welcome" stick on the top or bottom, opposite where the bow was placed. Encourage the participants to display their wreaths in a prominent place in their homes.

Welcoming New Neighbors

CONTRIBUTE TO THE NEEDS OF THE SAINTS; EXTEND HOSPITALITY TO STRANGERS.

Romans 12:13

LEARN

On the average, Americans move eleven times during their lifetimes. Many communities have welcoming organizations to help newly settled residents feel more at home. Maps, discount coupons, and other gifts are usually a part of the package. When a community opens its heart to accept new people, those who were once strangers are no longer so alone. In this activity the participants will contribute to this welcoming of new neighbors by making pin punched hearts as gifts for new people in the community.

LOCATE

- Yarn, 8" pieces
- White construction paper
- 3" cardboard heart patterns
- Scissors
- Hand towels, dish towels, or washcloths
- Pins, dressmaking pins or longer
- Paper punch
- One sample completed punched heart project
- Pencils

ADVANCE PREPARATION

- Cut the yarn in 8" pieces and one cardboard heart pattern for each participant.
- Prepare a completed pin punched heart for display.

LEAD

Discuss with the participants the experience of moving from one town or neighborhood to another. Ask: "What does it feel like to leave friends behind? What is it like to come to a new school and neighborhood where most everyone already knows one another? How does it feel when you meet your first friend in a new place? How does someone go about meeting a friend when they are new?" Also, ask the participants to share about a time when they befriended a person who was new to their area.

Tell the participants that they will be making pin punched hearts to use in welcoming new people to their community, church, or school. Show the group a sample of the completed pin punched heart before they begin. Place a folded hand towel, dish towel, or washcloth at each place. Also, distribute white construction paper, a pencil, a 3" cardboard heart pattern, an 8" piece of yarn, and scissors to each participant. Instruct them to trace the heart pattern very lightly on the paper and to cut it out. (It is important that when cutting the hearts the participants do not make a fold in the paper. A fold will mar the appearance of this project.) Allow the students to cut out as many hearts as time allows.

The punched pattern is created by laying the heart on the folded towel or washcloth. Holding the heart steady with one hand, the pin is used in the other hand to lightly poke holes through the paper. Encourage the participants to be creative in designing the pattern(s) for their hearts. However, tell them not to press their hands too heavily on the hearts, or the surface will become bent and the pattern will not show up nicely. Use a hole punch to make a hole at the top of each heart. Have the students string the 8" piece of yarn through the hole for hanging.

When the hearts are completed, simple messages can also be written on them. Have the participants use sharp pencils to write friendly messages like, "Welcome!" "Hope you enjoy your new home!" or "Welcome to (*name of town or church community*)."

There are many ways to distribute the hearts. They can be delivered to the homes of new people in the neighborhood or church community, at a senior citizen residence, or a newly completed apartment complex, or they can be given to new children at school. Make sure that an adult is present when the students distribute their hearts.

Close the session with a prayer as the participants each hold a heart. Ask them to pray for the people who will receive the hearts. Allow the participants to pray in their own words for people who are in need of hospitality and welcome.

Putting Out the Welcome Mat

WHEN SHE AND HER HOUSEHOLD WERE BAPTIZED, SHE URGED US, SAYING, "IF YOU HAVE JUDGED ME TO BE FAITHFUL TO THE LORD, COME AND STAY AT MY HOME." AND SHE PREVAILED UPON US.

Acts 16:15

LEARN

The nervousness, tension, and anxiety associated with being a stranger is experienced by all people at certain times; whether on a first day of school, moving into a neighborhood, at camp, on vacation, or while attempting a new activity. For this project, the participants will cover a door with paper and write messages and greetings in graffiti-style to help others feel more welcome.

LOCATE

✎ Door

✎ Butcher paper, long enough to cover the door on one or both sides

✎ Tape

✎ Glue

✎ Scissors

✎ Markers or crayons

✎ Dictionary

✎ Magazines or catalogs (optional)

ADVANCE PREPARATION

✎ Cover a door with butcher paper. Depending on the size of the group, one or both sides of the door may be covered.

✎ Print the letters "W-E-L-C-O-M-E" vertically down the center of the paper on the door's outer side.

LEAD

As the participants arrive, invite them to gather around the covered door. After everyone has assembled, read the dictionary definition of the word welcome to the group. Ask: "When was a time you felt welcomed? When was a time you felt unwelcomed?" Allow everyone a chance to share one example for each question. Tell the participants they are going to list things on the door that people can do to make another person feel welcome. Brainstorm a few phrases to use to express feeling welcomed such as a wave, a phone call, or sharing a face-to-face conversation. These ideas can be incorporated on the mural door in a number of ways, including:

1. The participants can write the words or phrases that begin with or include the letters of the word "welcome";

2. The participants can compose their own words and phrases and write them directly on the door;

3. The participants can draw pictures to express the welcoming theme.

Provide markers or crayons. Also, appropriate magazine photos may be glued to the door.

When the group has finished, comment on the words, phrases, and illustrations they have included on the door. Encourage the participants to share the graffiti door with others (for example, parents, friends, or children in other classes) in the next few days or weeks.

Feeling at Home

"BUT WE HAD TO CELEBRATE AND REJOICE, BECAUSE THIS
BROTHER OF YOURS WAS DEAD AND HAS COME TO LIFE;
HE WAS LOST AND HAS BEEN FOUND."

Luke 15:32

LEARN

Conflicts and unresolved arguments lead to separation. Even people living in the same home can become strangers to one another. A husband and wife stop talking, a father does not have the time to spend with his son, a sister carries a permanent grudge against her brother. In this activity the participants will role play situations that often occur in families as a way to elicit comments, ideas, and solutions to family problems.

LOCATE

- Copy of Resource 3A, "Conflict Situations"
- Basket, bag, or other container
- Bible

ADVANCE PREPARATION

- Duplicate Resource 3A and cut to separate the individual situations.
- Put the separated situation strips in a basket, bag, or other container.

LEAD

Assign these parts for a dramatic reading of the parable of the Prodigal Son (Lk 15:11–32): *Jesus (the narrator), younger son, father,* and *older son.* After the reading, discuss each character of the Bible story. Ask: "What caused the relationships to become strained? How were the broken relationships repaired?" Allow volunteers the chance to comment.

Next, focus the discussion on contemporary family life. Tell the participants that they will be acting out situations that occur in families today. Divide the group into smaller groups of two to three participants each. Have a representative from each group choose a slip and share it with the others. Allow time for each group to prepare a presentation of their situation. Then, have the small groups take turns presenting their scenes to the entire group.

After each presentation, ask volunteers to add comments, ideas, or solutions on the theme presented. Allow the participants the opportunity to talk about how the situations relate to their own family experience, however direct the conversation away from especially sensitive or personal topics.

Learning about Others

THE TWO ANGELS CAME TO SODOM IN THE EVENING, AND LOT WAS SITTING IN THE GATEWAY OF SODOM. WHEN LOT SAW THEM, HE ROSE TO MEET THEM, AND BOWED DOWN WITH HIS FACE TO THE GROUND.

Genesis 19:1

LEARN

Every country of the world has its own traditions of expressing hospitality and welcome. Some of these traditions may seem very strange to people who have not grown up with them or experienced them before. For this lesson the participants will play a game that will help them explore some customs of welcome from different nations and cultures.

LOCATE

✎ Copies of Resource 3B, "Hospitality Matching Game"

✎ Pencils

✎ Resource materials on various countries and customs

ADVANCE PREPARATION

✎ Duplicate one copy of Resource 3B for each participant.

LEAD

Play a matching guessing game to learn more about customs of welcome throughout the world. Distribute copies of Resource 3B, "Hospitality Matching Game" to each participant. Explain that the statements in the left column are to be matched with the words in the right column that name an item used to express hospitality. Remind the students that these are just guesses! The point of the game is simply to present some of the unique welcoming customs from around the world. When everyone has made their choices, share the correct answers.

If you wish to extend the activity, assign individuals or small groups to research more information on these or other welcoming customs from around the world.

Answers: (1) D; (2) H; (3) B; (4) F; (5) A; (6) G; (7) C; (8) E.

Singing the Language of Love

BELOVED, LET US LOVE ONE ANOTHER, BECAUSE LOVE IS FROM GOD; EVERYONE WHO LOVES IS BORN OF GOD AND KNOWS GOD.

1 John 4:7

LEARN

Amor. Liebe. Szeretet. All of these words mean love, yet no words are necessary to communicate the true meaning of love to others. There are many songs which emphasize this theme. One appropriate song is called "Love in Any Language."[1] This activity asks you to teach a song of love to the participants and to have the young people construct mobiles depicting the message of the music. In working through and completing this project the participants will expand their outlook and consider more people in the world to whom they can show love.

LOCATE

- Copies of the lyrics of the song of love you select
- Chalkboard and chalk or butcher paper and marker (optional)
- Copies of Resource 3C, "Many Ways to Say Love"
- Keyboard or guitar
- Magazines
- Scissors
- Glue
- Hole punch
- Yarn or ribbon, cut in 6" strips
- Poster board
- Wire hangers
- Markers

ADVANCE PREPARATION

- Display or distribute copies of the song lyrics to each participant.
- Duplicate one copy of Resource 3C for each participant.
- Arrange for a musician to accompany the choral singing on keyboard or guitar.

LEAD

Jesus' instruction to his disciples can be summarized in one word: love. Regardless of the relationship (with neighbors, classmates, family members, or strangers), Jesus commands people to love one another. Share the passage from 1 John 4:7 with the participants.

Help the participants realize the importance of showing love for all people of the world by teaching them a song that expresses the theme of love. "Love in Any Language" is especially appropriate though there are many songs that would work well (see below for more suggestions). Display or give copies of the lyrics to each person. Arrange for the musical accompanist to help with the rehearsal. If you wish, you may choose individual participants to sing verses as solos and the entire group to sing the chorus.

Add another dimension to the project. Tell the group that they will be making individual mobiles to illustrate the words for love in many different languages. Distribute Resource 3C, "Many Ways to Say Love," to each participant. Have the students try to guess the pronunciations of each of these words. Ask volunteers to share any other words for love that they may know.

For the individual mobiles, have each participant select four to six languages to illustrate. Distribute poster board, scissors, and markers. Tell them to cut out a variety of shapes from their paper and to write love in a different language on each piece. Provide magazines (*National Geographic*, travel magazines, and the like) and have the participants locate photos of people and places from the countries represented by the languages on their mobiles. These photos can be cut out and attached to the back side of the appropriate poster board shape. Punch a hole at the top of each shape and have the participants thread a 6" length of ribbon or yarn through it. Finally, have them tie each shape to a wire hanger.

Additional or alternate songs to use with this activity include:

◇ "Jesu, Jesu, Fill Us with Your Love"
(Ghana, Melody and Words, Jane M. Marshall, Arranger, and Tom Colvin, Translator. *Sing to God: Songs and Hymns for Christian Education*. New York: United Church Press, 1984.)

◇ "Love, Love, Love"
(Brokering, Lois and Herbert. *Little Ones Sing Praise*. St. Louis: Concordia, 1989.)

◇ "They'll Know We Are Christians by Our Love"
(Scholtes, Peter. *Songs and Hymns of Praise and Worship*. Grand Rapids, MI: Singspiration Music/Zondervan, 1974.)

◇ "We Love"
(Price, Ann F. *Little Ones Sing Praise*. St. Louis: Concordia, 1989.)

----

1 Mohr, Jon and John Mays. "Love in Any Language." Chatsworth, CA: Birdwing Music/Sutton Hill Music (The Sparrow Corporation). 1985.

Offering a Prayer

THEN SHE FELL PROSTRATE, WITH HER FACE TO THE GROUND, AND SAID TO HIM, "WHY HAVE I FOUND FAVOR IN YOUR SIGHT, THAT YOU SHOULD TAKE NOTICE OF ME, WHEN I AM A FOREIGNER?"

Ruth 2:10

LEARN

People become strangers due to many situations within and beyond their control. In this activity, the participants will examine some of these unexpected ways that people become strangers to one another and discover one way they can help to alleviate many of these situations.

LOCATE

- Newspaper and magazine articles and photos that illustrate people who are anxious or alone because of things like a natural disaster, being new in a strange land, or travelling on business
- Chalkboard or newsprint
- Chalk or marker
- Construction paper
- Scissors
- Markers
- Pencils
- Metal rings or paper clips
- Hole punch

LEAD

Display newspaper and magazine articles and photographs that illustrate people who have become unexpected strangers. Ask the students to comment on the subject matter of the articles and the facial expressions of the people in the photographs. Brainstorm with the students and record a list on the chalkboard of many of the ways in which people become strangers. The list might include examples like being displaced because of a natural disaster, travelling on vacation or business, being an exchange student in a foreign country, moving to a new place, or starting at a new school.

Regardless of the ways in which people become strangers, they need to experience God's love. One way for anyone to concern themselves with people who are strangers is prayer. Help the participants create a unique prayer and lead the group in a prayer activity that will help them to reach out to people in need who are both near and far.

Distribute the construction paper, pencils, scissors, and markers. Direct each participant to trace his or her hand on the paper, cut out the tracing, and write his or her name on the "palm" of the hand with a marker. Next, have the participants write P-R-A-Y on the tops of the four fingers, beginning with the little finger. Ask: "What are words or phrases that begin with each of these letters that describe how you show others God's love?" (for example, P—pray, R—reconcile hurts, A—advocate justice, Y—yearn for joy). Have each person choose similar words or phrases and write them on the fingers.

When the hands have been completed, punch a hole at the top and bottom of each shape. Gather the group in a circle and invite each person, in turn, to offer his or her prayer. Link all of the hands together with paper clips to form a prayer chain. Hang the chain in the room. Encourage the participants to remember in their prayers during the upcoming week those who are strangers because of unexpected circumstances.

Showing Kindness to All

DO NOT NEGLECT TO SHOW HOSPITALITY TO STRANGERS,
FOR BY DOING THAT SOME HAVE ENTERTAINED ANGELS
WITHOUT KNOWING IT.

Hebrews 13:2

LEARN

Adapted from a Leo Tolstoy short story, "Martin the Cobbler" has become a classic tale. It tells the story of Martin, an old cobbler, who has lost his family and all interest in living. Then, in a dream, he is inspired by a voice, which he believes is the Lord's, promising to visit him the next day. By evening his "special guest" has not arrived, even though several needy people have come to his door and sought and received his aid. That night as he reads the scriptures a vision reveals to Martin that in caring for others he has met Jesus. Renewed and joyful again, Martin joins his old friends in celebrating the winter festival. Follow the directions for turning this tale into a puppet play. Invite guests to the presentation to help the participants better share the importance of caring for others.

LOCATE

- "Martin the Cobbler"[1] video or "Where Love Is, God Is"[2] story or tape
- VCR and monitor (optional)
- 3" to 5" diameter Styrofoam balls
- Plastic tubs
- Poly foam carpet pad
- Dowel rods or chopsticks
- 6" strips of panty hose
- Felt
- Fabric
- Yarn or fake fur
- Trims (optional)
- Glue
- Scissors
- Exacto knife
- Needles
- Thread
- Tape
- Sample puppet

LEAD

Show the video, play the cassette, or read the story of "Martin the Cobbler" to the group. Then help the participants to make puppets that can be used in a presentation of the tale. Puppets for the following characters need to be made: *Martin, the three strangers who visit him,* and the *townspeople.*

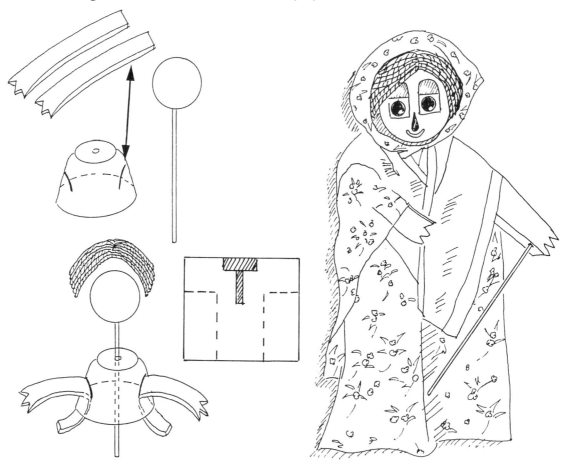

The body parts of the puppets are made from several recyclable objects. A Styrofoam ball forms the head, panty hose becomes the skin, and a plastic margarine or frozen whipping cream tub serves as the shoulders. Strips of carpet pad turn into two arms and the chopstick or dowel rod becomes the rod by which the puppet is operated. Assign various students to work on one or more of the puppets. Have the participants follow these directions to put the pieces of each puppet together:

> Insert the dowel rod into the bottom of the Styrofoam ball. After the hole is made, remove the rod. Spread glue on one edge of the rod and reinsert the rod into the hole. After it dries, cut a small hole into the bottom of the plastic tub. Also cut a small slit on each side of the tub. Cut arms from the poly foam carpet pad and fit one into each side slit. Take a six-inch length of panty hose. Tie off one of the loose ends, pull the piece over the ball, and tie the other end of the panty hose around the stick with a strip of yarn. Using felt scraps, cut out eyes, nose, and mouth. Glue them to the puppet's

head. Choose yarn or fake fur to make hair. Glue the hair to the top of the puppet's head. Insert the rod into the hole in the top of the plastic container. Pull the panty hose through the hole, and tape it to the stick. Place a large piece of tape under the plastic carton to hold up the container. Choose a piece of fabric for the costume. Cut a hole into the center of the fabric, and slide it over the puppet's head. Sew the material tightly around the neck. Make a few stitches on each side of the piece underneath the puppet's arms. Add trims as desired to complete the costume. Insert another dowel rod into one of the puppet's hands. To operate the character, hold the rod under the costume in one hand, and work the rod on the arm with the other hand.

You may wish to demonstrate each step as the group works on their own puppets or simply show them your completed puppet. In either case, allow appropriate time between each step. If possible, arrange for some additional adult volunteers to be present and assist those students who need help.

After the puppets are completed, assign roles, practice the play, and perform it for other classes, the entire congregation, or community groups.

---

1 In video format, "Martin the Cobbler" is available from: Mass Media Ministries, 2116 North Charles Street, Baltimore, MD 21218; (410) 727-3270. Running time: 27 minutes.
2 Tolstoy, Leo. "Where Love Is, God Is." *What Men Live By: Russian Stories*. New York: Pantheon, 1943.
    The story is also available as a paperback book and a cassette tape, from: Sandpiper Press, P.O. Box 286, Brookings, OR 97415; (513) 459-5588.

Blessings of a Stranger

THEN HE WAITED ANOTHER SEVEN DAYS, AND SENT OUT
THE DOVE; AND IT DID NOT RETURN TO HIM ANY MORE.

Genesis 8:12

LEARN

There are many examples in the Bible of people who welcomed and provided for the needs of sojourners. In these examples, not only did the sojourners benefit from the kindly actions, but God also blessed the person who was willing to help or be accepting! Though these people did not do an act of kindness to receive a blessing, God did something special for them all the same. Through answering riddles the participants will uncover more about the people who shared and received God's blessings in helping others.

LOCATE

✎ Copies of Resource 3D, "Scripture Riddles"

✎ Pencils

✎ Bibles

ADVANCE PREPARATION

✎ Duplicate one copy of Resource 3D for each participant.

LEAD

Discuss giving and receiving through the act of welcoming another. Ask: "When was a time you reached out to someone who was lonely, new to school or neighborhood, or in need of a friend? What benefit did the person receive from your actions? What benefit or blessing did you receive by acting as you did?" Allow volunteers the chance to share their experiences with the group.

Next, distribute copies of Resource 3D, "Scripture Riddles," to each participant. Explain that these riddles can be solved by looking up citations in the Bible, however, they are first to guess answers by only using the riddle clues themselves. These guesses should be written on the appropriate lines. Then, have the participants work in pairs to check their answers in the Bible. Have them write the correct answers on the second line. After both steps are completed, check and discuss the passages and correct answers with the entire group.

Answers: 1. Abraham and Sarah; 2. Rachel; 3. A widow; 4. Shunammite woman; 5. Joseph and Mary; 6. Lazaras, Martha, and Mary; 7. The good Samaritan; 8. Lydia.

Making New Friends

FOR THERE IS NOTHING HIDDEN, EXCEPT TO BE DIS-
CLOSED; NOR IS ANYTHING SECRET, EXCEPT TO COME TO
LIGHT.

Mark 4:22

LEARN

In the parable of the lamp, Jesus asks, "Is a lamp brought in to be put under the bushel basket, or under the bed, and not on the lampstand?" (Mk 4:21). The good news of Jesus is to be embraced and shared with others. In this movement activity the participants will experience and appreciate the invitation and acceptance of being a member of God's people.

LOCATE

✎ Newsprint or chalkboard

✎ Markers or chalk

ADVANCE PREPARATION

✎ Write the words to the "Friendship Song" on the chalkboard or a piece of newsprint placed where all can see.

✎ Arrange for a group of younger children (grades K–3) to join your group for this song activity.

LEAD

If possible, arrange for your group to lead younger children (grades K–3) in this song movement. Divide the group of younger children into small groups ranging from one member to six members (make sure the number sung in the last verse corresponds with the number of children in the largest group). Intersperse older students into the small groups of younger children. Have all the participants sit in a circle on the floor. If there is a large number of people in the large group, form several circles, or have several smaller groups within the same circle.

Point out the words to the "Friendship Song." Sing or hum the tune to the song "Three Blind Mice." Tell the group that the "Friendship Song" is sung to the same tune. Choose a leader to walk around the circle as the first verse of the "Friendship Song" is sung. At the point of the song "Come with me," the leader chooses one person to join with him or her. The singing continues and the appropriate number of children are added for each verse.

Repeat the entire song several times, changing the groups and giving more of the older participants the opportunity to be leaders. You may also have the leaders add a new action for each verse to go along with their walking and singing. Suggestions: skipping, hopping, twirling, trotting, or side-step!

The Friendship Song

I am one. I am one.
I'm having fun. I'm having fun.
Now let's see what we can do
Come with me and we'll make it two.
We are two. We are two.

We are two. We are two.
Look what we can do. Look what we can do.
Come with us and you can see
We can turn two into three.
We are three. We are three.

We are three. We are three.
Happy as can be. Happy as can be.
Come with us and make one more.
So we'll have a group of four.
We are four. We are four.

We are four. We are four.
Let's add more. Let's add more.
Come with us and make it five.
Celebrate that we're alive.
We are five. We are five.

We are five. We are five.
Glad to be alive. Glad to be alive.
Come with us and we'll all mix.
Now we have a group of six.
We are six. We are six.

Come along. Come along.
Sing our song. Sing our song.
When you reach out to make a friend
You'll be happy in the end.
We are friends. We are friends.

FOUR

I was poor

Overview

Poverty—the lack of sufficient food, clothing, shelter, medicines, and education—is never far from view. Not only has television brought every corner of the world live into our homes, but the homeless, needy, and deprived can be seen on the streets of most any community in the country. Jesus prediction—"You always have the poor with you" (Jn 12:8)—is certainly true.

However, Jesus did not just point out the poor and the conditions of the poor. He gave his disciples instructions for caring for the poor's material needs. For example, in Matthew 25:36, Jesus said: "I was naked and you gave me clothing." When you care for the physical needs of the poor, you are doing it for Jesus. The activities in this chapter will help the participants discover ways of helping the poor that can develop into habits that may continue for the rest of their lives.

Also, because people can be spiritually as well as physically poor, the needs of the "poor in spirit" will also be addressed. Jesus pointed out the spiritually poor in the first beatitude delivered at the Sermon on the Mount (see Mt 5:3). Other activities will specifically help the students to recognize and meet the needs of the poor in spirit and help to bring the fullness of God's kingdom one step closer to realization.

Clothing the Poor

ALL THE WIDOWS STOOD BESIDE HIM, WEEPING AND SHOWING TUNICS AND OTHER CLOTHING THAT DORCAS HAD MADE WHILE SHE WAS WITH THEM.

Acts 9:39

LEARN

Dorcas, also known as Tabitha, was a disciple in the early church who, according to the Acts of the Apostles, made and repaired clothing to be given to the poor, especially widows and orphans. In this activity the participants will discover how clothing ministries continue in their own community and church. They will make a rag doll to reinforce the lesson that clothing materials can be used over and over in many different ways.

LOCATE

- ✎ 10" muslin squares or other off-white or white material which does not ravel easily
- ✎ Scissors
- ✎ 1/8" X 10" lengths of satin ribbon
- ✎ Fibre fill
- ✎ Embroidery floss and needles, puff paints, fabric paints, or paint markers (optional)

- ✎ Small satin roses (optional)
- ✎ Glue (optional)
- ✎ Chalkboard or newsprint
- ✎ Chalk or marker
- ✎ Phone book or social service directory

ADVANCE PREPARATION

- ✎ Prepare a list of local and regional agencies that assist in clothing distribution.

LEAD

Read or summarize the story of Dorcas from Acts 9:36-41. Then ask: "What are some clothing ministries you are aware of in your church or community today?" List the suggestions on a chalkboard or a piece of newsprint. Also, share a list of agencies that clothe the poor (for example, the Salvation Army, Goodwill Industries, Saint Vincent de Paul, or thrift shops operated by local churches).

Ask: "Who or where do you pass on your clothing to after you have grown out of it?" Allow time for sharing. Then point out that any clothing can be reused in some way. Charities that collect clothing distribute or sell the wearable goods to people who need it. The worn-out clothes are sold to manufacturing companies who turn them into rag stuffing for toys and other items. Also, the money the charitable organizations receive for the clothes is used to aid various ministry outreaches to the poor.

Next, explain that in colonial times fabric and other resources were scarce and used clothing was gathered to make rag or handkerchief dolls. Today, variations of rag dolls are made in many different regions of the United States, including Appalachia. Tell the students that they will make a simple rag doll to better understand how clothing materials can be recycled.

For the project itself, assign the students a work space at a table. Give a 10" square piece of muslin or other white or off-white fabric to each participant. Say: "Lay the fabric in front of you in a shape like a diamond." Distribute a small amount of fibre fill to each person. Then demonstrate how to make the head by stuffing a small amount of fibre fill into one corner of the fabric and gathering the fabric around it. The corner of the fabric should be tied in place with a double knot using a thin ribbon. Allow the long ends of the ribbon to hang down the remaining portion of the fabric. Tie a bow with the long pieces. If possible, glue a satin rose to the center of the bow. Pause and help the participants with these steps before proceeding.

The hands of the doll can be formed in one of two ways: either take the side points of the square and tie each in a small knot or gather the points and tie each in place with a small piece of thin ribbon (make a double knot). Explain that the faces of the colonial rag dolls were traditionally left blank.

To extend the activity, invite the participants to sew a simple running stitch along the lower edge of the "dress." Puff paints, fabric paints, or paint markers can also be used to make a decorative border.

Remind the participants that these rag dolls are one way that clothing materials can be reused. If you wish, the group can sell their finished projects to members of the congregation and donate any proceeds to agencies that work to meet the needs of the poor.

Expressing the Pain

TURN TO ME AND BE GRACIOUS TO ME, FOR I AM LONELY AND AFFLICTED.

Psalm 25:16

LEARN

The lament psalms are filled with examples of voices crying out to God. Lament psalms are those that call attention to the human condition of sorrow through the expression of weeping or wailing. The phrases "Why?" "How long?" and "Hear my cry" are repeated frequently. Emotions like sadness, loneliness, fear, and sorrow are directed to God for a response. This activity will help the participants to identify ways in which people feel empty, lost, and lowly—especially when precious things like health, safety, or dignity are stripped from them. Through exploring the psalms and writing their own poetry or lament psalms, the participants will express their feelings of being poor in spirit and empathize with those same feelings in others.

LOCATE

✎ Bibles

✎ Paper

✎ Pencils

✎ Chalkboard or mural paper

✎ Chalk (colored, if possible) or markers

LEAD

Introduce the notion of lamenting or grieving by reading Psalm 25 to the participants. Provide bibles and ask the participants to search the book of Psalms to find other examples that express a person's lament (refer especially to Psalms 1—7). Then, assign each person a specific psalm or set of five psalms to scan for words that express sorrow or lament. Say:

As you find a word go to the chalkboard (or mural paper) and write it down. You can write or print your words in any style, angle, or color. Do not worry about keeping them in neat columns. Continue searching for more words until the entire space has been filled in.

When the board or mural is complete, lead a discussion based on these words. Point to a word and ask: "Who are the people who might feel this way today? What might have been taken from people to make them feel this way?" Possible situations of suffering include experiencing a severe illness, being physically, emotionally, or sexually abused, being robbed or attacked, or committing a serious sin. List these situations on another area of the board or on a separate piece of butcher paper.

Next, ask the participants to write their own poems or lament psalms based on one of the situations on the list. Encourage them to write from the perspective of the person who is experiencing the difficulty. Remind them to direct their psalms to God. If you wish, suggest that some or all of these phrases be incorporated in their work:

O God . . .
Why . . .
How . . .
Help me . . .
Hear my cry . . .
Listen to me . . .
O Lord, you . . .

When the poems or laments are complete, allow each to be read either by the person who wrote it or by another person in the group. Allow time for a discussion of the theme and for the group to offer specific prayer intentions for those experiencing difficulty in their lives.

Becoming Personally Involved

THEY WOULD SELL THEIR POSSESSIONS AND GOODS AND DISTRIBUTE THE PROCEEDS TO ALL, AS ANY HAD NEED.

Acts 2:45

LEARN

From the earliest history of the church, there have been many examples of people who have devoted their entire lives and spent all of their resources to help the poor. Many of these people—including Dorothy Day, Martin Luther King Jr., and Mother Teresa in this century—have lived dramatic and well-known lives because of their service. Other people, including those you may know from your own experience, have given tirelessly, albeit without fanfare, to help those less fortunate. In this activity you are asked to share a story of someone who has been personally involved in ministering to others in Jesus' name and to encourage the participants to do the same.

LOCATE

- Bible
- Periodical articles and biographical information of persons who minister to the poor
- Paper
- Pens or pencils
- Costume pieces (optional)
- Props (optional)

LEAD

Tell two stories, one of a well-known contemporary person who is known for his or her service to the poor and the other of someone you know from your personal experience who likewise provides aid to those in need. Use any creative method (perhaps a first person format; for example, "I am Dorothy Day . . .") to tell the stories of their words and actions.

Next, have the participants prepare a similar presentation. Say:

> You are to prepare first person stories about ordinary people who do extraordinary things. About people who, with God's help, minister to the needy.

Explain that a first person story, or monologue, is a dramatic narrative portrayed by one actor and is usually written in the present tense. Though monologues may be performed without lights, scenery, props, or costumes, encourage the students to look for ways to incorporate these "extras" into their presentations in order to add another worthwhile dimension.

Provide resource materials, such as magazine or newspaper articles or biographies of people who minister to the poor. Invite each group member to select a person to use as the basis of a report. With your approval, the participants may also select a person whom they have encountered in their own experience to report on. Distribute paper and pens or pencils and allow time for the gathering of facts and the writing of the monologues. Contribute additional information and give help where needed. If costumes and props are accessible, make them available to the actors.

Invite each participant to present a first person story to the group. Limit the time of each monologue to three minutes. At the conclusion of the monologues, offer a prayer of thanks for all people who demonstrate care and concern for the poor.

Searching for Support

SO FAITH BY ITSELF, IF IT HAS NO WORKS, IS DEAD.

James 2:17

LEARN

Estimates indicate that one out of every five children in America lives in poverty. Solving the problem on an individual and collective basis demands creative responses by people of faith. The words of James 2:14-17 challenge every Christian to get involved! In this scavenger hunt activity the participants will discover community support groups and services available to people with special needs.

LOCATE

✎ Copies of Resource 4A, "Scavenger Hunt List"

✎ Telephone directories, one for each team

✎ Brochures with information on service agencies for the poor, one for each team

ADVANCE PREPARATION

✎ Duplicate one copy of Resource 4A for each participant.

✎ Arrange transportation and adult chaperons for scavenger hunt (optional).

LEAD

Gather the participants and brainstorm a list of materials, services, and support systems that people with substandard income require (for example, counseling, advocacy, housing, clothing, food, medical treatment, and friendship). Also ask where people might go to meet these needs (for example, health departments, youth centers, food pantries, clothing distribution points, and after-school care programs).

Tell the students that they will be participating in a scavenger hunt to locate service and support groups available to the poor. Determine the procedure for your scavenger hunt. Items 1-7 on the "Scavenger Hunt List" can be "gathered" without leaving your site by using the telephone book and making phone calls and by looking through newspapers, magazines, and brochures and finding names of agencies. Items 8-10 (optional) need to be gathered by actually going to suggested sites.

Assign the individuals to teams. If the teams are leaving the site, arrange for one adult per five students to accompany them. Distribute Resource 4A and review the items together so that the participants understand what they are being asked to do.

Before beginning the scavenger hunt, review guidelines, set a time limit, share information about locations, provide resources like phone books and agency brochures, and answer any questions that will clarify the procedure.

When the teams have finished, have one representative from each group share the group's results. Compile all of the information into a resource file for your future use.

Encouraging Through Music

THEREFORE ENCOURAGE ONE ANOTHER AND BUILD UP
EACH OTHER, AS INDEED YOU ARE DOING.

1 Thessalonians 5:11

LEARN

A person who has been robbed of his or her dignity can be considered poor. Feelings of self-worth and acceptance are treasures which should be protected. Young people often struggle to feel valued. As much as they need self-worth and acceptance, however, many youth are often unwilling to help others in their personal growth. Rather, negative comments, put-downs, and criticism are too often the order of the day. In fact, positive and negative messages have many sources, one of them being music lyrics. In this activity the participants will share a variety of music which affects their spirits in both uplifting and defeating ways.

LOCATE

✎ Cassette tape and/or CD player

✎ Tapes and/or CDs of secular and Christian music

ADVANCE PREPARATION

✎ Collect contemporary tapes and CDs that include both positive and negative musical lyrics. You may wish to assign the participants to bring at least one example of each type of music to the scheduled session.

LEAD

Read I Thessalonians 5:11. Discuss common disparaging remarks that are made by young people. Ask: "How does it make you feel when someone puts you down?" Have the group contrast those feelings with how it feels to be encouraged or affirmed by another person.

Spend time sharing the tapes and CDs which were brought by the students. Allow each participant to share and explain the songs or parts of songs that communicate their uniqueness and value. Next, have the students play the songs with negative lyrics. These would include lyrics that represent a lack of value for life, present people as sex objects, or devalue a particular ethnic or religious group. Ask: "How do these words make you feel? How do these lyrics rob people of their dignity?"

Select a positive song to play as a conclusion to the presentation. Challenge each person to choose music that will minister positively to their spirits, build their sense of self-worth, and enable them to use their gifts in service of others.

Addressing Unemployment Issues

LET THE FAVOR OF THE LORD OUR GOD BE UPON US, AND PROSPER FOR US THE WORK OF OUR HANDS—O PROSPER THE WORK OF OUR HANDS!

Psalm 90:17

LEARN

Addressing issues concerning unemployment is an important aspect of learning to minister to the poor. Many of the themes and experiences related to unemployment are common among all people who face that difficulty. In this activity the participants will learn more about the factors facing the unemployed by conducting surveys and using the information they collect to weave place mats. They will also remember the unemployed in prayer.

LOCATE

- Paper
- Pencils
- Construction paper (one 12" X 18" piece for each participant; several 1" X 12" strips for each participant)
- Scissors
- Paper cutter (optional)
- Ruler
- Glue
- Masking tape or tacks
- Chalkboard or newsprint
- Chalk or markers

ADVANCE PREPARATION

- Cut construction paper into 1" x 12" strips.

LEAD

Introduce the theme of the session and read the passage from Psalm 90:17. Tell the participants that they will be taking surveys to determine common issues related to unemployment. Explain that a survey is an information gathering tool that records opinions, but not necessarily facts. Distribute paper and pencils. Discuss basic questions related to the unemployment issue. Have the participants list one or two of these questions on their papers; for example, "What are some problems faced by the unemployed?" or "What do you feel is the major cause of unemployment?" Instruct the participants to pose their questions to family members, friends, and members of the church community. If you wish to conduct the entire activity within one session you might arrange for another group from your congregation to be present and serve as a test group for the survey.

Ask the participants to share the results of the surveys when completed. Record common themes of the responses on the chalkboard or newsprint. Themes might include loss of dignity, uncertain plans, and lack of finances. Allow the participants time to share their impressions of the surveying process.

Next, distribute materials for the weaving activity. Explain that each person is to choose several unemployment issues and themes and write them with a marker on the 1" x 12" strips of paper. Through weaving these strips together the participants will discover that the various components of unemployment are interconnected. Encourage variety in the selection of issues and themes.

Demonstrate this procedure for making the woven mat. Have the participants follow along:

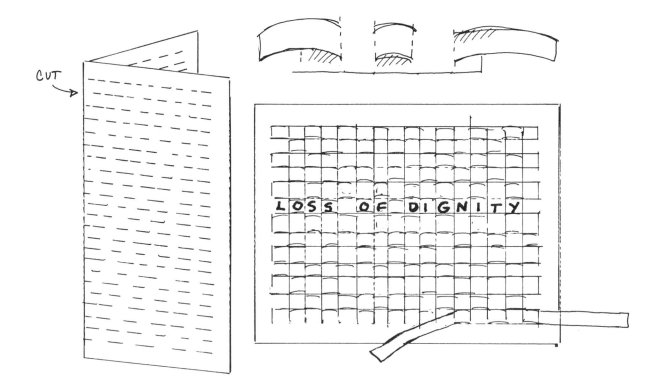

First, fold a 12" x 18" piece of construction paper in half horizontally. Lightly mark a margin line with pencil one inch from an open edge of the paper, opposite the fold. Cut slits into the folded edge, spacing them one inch apart. Be certain to stop cutting at the margin line. Next, open the paper and lay it flat. Begin weaving the strips with unemployment issues and themes under and over the slits in the paper. Alternate each row. If row one starts with an under lap then start row two with an overlap. Continue until the colored strips are woven across the entire width of the paper, forming a mat. Fasten the loose ends of the strips with glue.

Pause to help the participants as needed or have them work in pairs so each partner can help the other.

Tape or tack the completed mats to a bulletin board or wall. Ask each participant to stand near his or her project and share reflections on the problem of unemployment with the rest of the group. Also, have the students take turns offering one sentence prayers for people affected by unemployment; for example, "I pray for the family that does not have money for a home." Ask the participants to take their weavings home, to use them as placemats or table decorations, and to continue remembering unemployed people in their daily prayers.

Giving for the Poor

A POOR WIDOW CAME AND PUT IN TWO SMALL COPPER COINS, WHICH ARE WORTH A PENNY.

Mark 12:42

LEARN

How many times do people pass by a penny in the street because it is "not worth the trouble" to stop and pick up? Yet, the poor widow's simple offering of two coins of less value was worth more than all other contributions. This activity will help the students learn about organizations that use pennies to help the poor. Also, the participants will plan skits about people who have been helped by these various organizations.

LOCATE

✎ Small paper bag

✎ Pennies, enough to fill one small paper bag

ADVANCE PREPARATION

✎ Fill a small paper bag with pennies.

✎ Arrange for the participants to present their skits to an outside audience (optional).

LEAD

Have the group sit in a circle on the floor. Hold up a bag filled with pennies but tell the students that it is a bag of seeds. Shake the bag and ask: "What kind of seeds do you think these are?" When someone guesses that the "seeds" are really pennies, show the group a handful and tell them that, like seeds, pennies can be used to grow many wonderful things. Explain that many charitable organizations take and combine penny contributions and use them to support projects which help poor people in many different ways.

Read Mark 12:41-44 to the group. Say, "Just like the widow who only had two small coins, it only takes a penny given in love to make a big difference!" Then summarize the efforts of the following charitable organizations and any others you wish to include:

1. **UNICEF (United Nations International Children's Emergency Fund)** provides free immunizations and vaccines for children around the world as well as many other kinds of medical help for children who would otherwise not receive it. The penny donations collected from programs like "Halloween Trick or Treating for UNICEF" helps support the group's efforts around the world.

2. **Project Heifer** uses pennies to purchase livestock that can be raised as a food source. Poor people living in rural areas are given animals like sheep, chickens, cows, or goats that can be bred and passed on to another family in need.

3. Many social and service groups from all over the world participate in a program called "Least Coin." These groups collect their nation's "least coin" from members at each meeting. At the end of the year these donations are pooled together and represent quite a large sum. The money is used on such things as providing medicine and education for poor and developing nations.

4. Many local churches sponsor their own projects. The Community Church in Harrignton Park, New Jersey has several different programs to collect small change. For "Thankful for Teeth," volunteers paid a dime for each of their teeth to thank God for this blessing. A dentist from the community used the collected money for supplies needed to help children who couldn't afford dental care. The "Change for Change Challenge" program encouraged the congregation to fill a large container with coins that when laid out would stretch one mile. The money was used to help rebuild a house for a family in Appalachia.

After the presentation, divide the participants into small groups of four to five people each. Tell them that each group is to develop a skit based on the experiences of people who have been helped by the pennies collected by others. Suggest or assign one of the following themes or have the groups develop one of their own. Examples include:

◇ children who were given life-saving and protecting immunizations by UNICEF;

◇ a family who received a calf from Project Heifer;

◇ children attending a school built by Least Coin;

◇ a family living in a house built or fixed by people from a church.

Instruct the group members to plan their skits. Each person should have a hand in developing the story and participating in the production. Allow the groups time to practice the skits and present them to the other groups. Then, if possible, arrange for parents, members of the church community, or children in other classes to view the presentation. Ask for a coin donation. Choose one of the agencies studied and donate the profits to that group.

Celebrating the Caring

GIVE TO EVERYONE WHO BEGS FROM YOU; AND IF ANY-
ONE TAKES AWAY YOUR GOODS, DO NOT ASK FOR THEM
AGAIN.

Luke 6:30

LEARN

The practice of giving to others in Jesus' name is a requirement of Christian discipleship. Saint Martin of Tours, a fourth century bishop in France, learned this lesson as a young boy. A legend repeated each year on November 11, Saint Martin's feast day, recalls the need to care for others. In this activity the participants will hear about Saint Martin and participate in a Martinmas celebration. They will create a party to celebrate the actions of Saint Martin and others who give their lives to help the poor.

LOCATE

- Unfrosted cupcakes, one for each participant
- Frosting
- Food coloring or fruit slices
- Juice
- Cups
- Napkins
- Plates
- Forks
- Candles
- Candle holders
- Matches

ADVANCE PREPARATION

- Prepare one bowl of white frosting and one bowl of orange or yellow frosting.

LEAD

Share this legend of Saint Martin of Tours that is retold and celebrated in France and other countries:

As a young man Martin passed through an archway in the city where he lived. Under the arch he saw a poor beggar shivering in the cold. The homeless man was almost naked, having few clothes to keep him warm. Martin took off his cape, tore it in half, and gave half of it to the poor man. The next night Martin had a dream in which Christ appeared. In Martin's dream, Jesus was wearing the piece of cape which Martin had given to the beggar! Then Martin understood that by helping the poorest of people he was really helping Christ. Martin became a bishop and is today the patron saint of beggars, outcasts, and the homeless. In France November 11 is known as Martinmas, or Saint Martin's feast day. His life is celebrated with a simple cake. Also, a festival of lanterns is held, with light carried throughout the rooms of a darkened house to recall how Saint Martin brought light to many people who experienced only darkness in their lives.

Have the participants share in preparing for your group's own celebration of Martinmas. Have the participants frost the cupcakes with white frosting. Then have them use the yellow or colored icing to create a sun image by spreading it over the white icing to create a design. Fruit slices can also be used to create the sun. Set the table for the party with napkins, plates, and cups. Pour cups of juice.

When the group is ready for the celebration, ask the participants to name other people who have dedicated their lives to helping the poor. Light a candle as a symbol for each person mentioned and set it in the center of the table. Just before serving the cupcakes, read Luke 6:30-31 as an opening prayer. Enjoy the treat the group has created together.

Responding to Needs

FOR MACEDONIA AND ACHAIA HAVE BEEN PLEASED TO
SHARE THEIR RESOURCES WITH THE POOR AMONG THE
SAINTS AT JERUSALEM.

Romans 15:26

LEARN

Unfortunately, poverty often strikes unexpectedly. People are stripped of material possessions quickly as a hurricane strikes, in a matter of days as medical bills mount, or over the course of several years as retirement income declines. Paul's words in the letter to the Romans tell how the Gentile Christians in the early church shared their material possessions with the citizens of Jerusalem who faced difficult times following a famine. Through making a patchwork quilt that illustrates ways in which God's love is shared with people in need, the participants will become more aware of how they too can participate in this important ministry of service.

LOCATE

- Fabric, one 4" X 4" square piece per participant
- Scissors
- Permanent markers, paint markers, or liquid embroidery pens
- Sewing equipment

- Backing material (optional)
- *Wonder Under* (optional)
- Bible

ADVANCE PREPARATION

- Cut one 4" x 4" fabric square for each participant.
- Arrange for a parent or member of the local congregation or community to sew the completed fabric squares together to form a quilt (optional).

LEAD

Introduce the activity. Tell the participants that they will be working together to make a patchwork quilt that illustrates ways of sharing God's love with people in need. Read Romans 15:25-26. Explain that there had been a famine in Jerusalem. Paul was commending the Christian community for reaching out and meeting the needs of the hungry.

Brainstorm with the group about some of the different kinds of disasters today that befall people (for example, hurricanes, floods, tornados, accidents, illness, unemployment, and war). Next, have the participants work individually and each come up with one way that Christians can and do respond to meet the needs of people in the types of difficult situations that were mentioned. For example, if a person has lost a home because of a tornado, an organization such as Church World Service might repair the residence. Or, if a person has lost income and insurance because of terminal illness, local church community's may assist with hospice care. Remind the students to list specific solutions to specific disasters. The solutions will make up the content of each person's patchwork quilt square.

After each student has listed his or her own solution, distribute the fabric patches and the permanent markers, liquid embroidery pens, or paint markers. Tell the participants to decorate their squares with meaningful designs, scenes, symbols, or words to represent their solutions.

When the students have finished decorating the squares, determine how they will be arranged by having participants lay them out on the floor or large table. The patches can be formed into a quilt by sewing them together by hand or machine or ironing them onto a larger fabric background using a bonding material like *Wonder Under*.

Display the completed patchwork piece in a prominent place to remind the participants of their commitment and specific ways of sharing God's love with people in need. Or, if desired, arrange to auction the quilt to members of the congregation. Donate the profits to an organization that provides relief to those suffering the effects of sudden or long-term disasters.

Helping the Homeless

IS IT NOT TO SHARE YOUR BREAD WITH THE HUNGRY, AND BRING THE HOMELESS POOR INTO YOUR HOUSE; WHEN YOU SEE THE NAKED, TO COVER THEM, AND NOT TO HIDE YOURSELF FROM YOUR OWN KIN?

Isaiah 58:7

LEARN

Homelessness is a complex problem with many causes. People may become homeless because of unemployment, limited income, high housing costs, alcohol or drug abuse, divorce, a natural disaster, or a serious mental illness. This activity will help the participants explore the multi-faceted issue of homelessness and decide on a plan that can help solve this most difficult problem.

LOCATE

- *Benjamin Brody's Backyard Bag* (Wezeman, Phyllis Vos and Colleen Aalsburg Wiessner. Elgin, IL: Brethren Press, 1991.) (optional)
- Paper shopping bag with handles
- Markers
- Brown paper grocery bags
- Masking tape
- Printed resource information on homelessness

ADVANCE PREPARATION

- *Benjamin Brody's Backyard Bag* is a children's story on homelessness. It can be obtained at most libraries or bookstores, or directly from:
  Active Learning Associates, Inc.
  P.O. Box 1251
  Mishawaka, IN 46546
  219-255-3570.

LEAD

Display a large paper shopping bag with handles. Brainstorm with the participants some of the ways that the bag can be used (for example, carrying groceries or turning it into a costume). Use a marker to record their ideas on one side of the bag. If no one has mentioned that homeless people sometimes use a bag to carry their possessions, do so yourself. Point out that, in effect, the bag becomes the homeless person's home.

Read the book *Benjamin Brody's Backyard Bag* to the participants or summarize the story using the following script. Say:

> Once a little boy named Benjamin Brody discovered many creative uses for a grocery bag. The bag became a garage for his toy cars, a tablecloth for a picnic, and a net for catching butterflies. Once, on a walk with his mother and sister, Benjamin noticed a woman sitting on a park bench sorting through items in a large paper shopping bag of her own. Benjamin thought that she must be playing his game, too. When Benjamin spoke with the woman, however, he discovered that she was not playing a game. In fact, for her, the bag was a home.

After finishing the story, ask the participants to think of items that they could collect and place in the bag to help homeless people. Write their suggestions on the other side of the bag. Affirm their suggestions and encourage the participants to begin a collection of some of these items (for example, food, clothing, blankets, and toiletries) that can be donated to an agency that aids the homeless.

Next, distribute a brown paper grocery bag and markers to each participant. Have them use the markers to divide the bag into four equal sections. Say:

> Write one of the following words in each quarter of the bag: *World, Nation, State,* and *Community*. Next, draw a cartoon, words, or symbols in each section that illustrates one solution for homelessness on the world, national, state, or community scale.

You may wish to share these examples:

◇ **World**: Church World Service collects blankets that are distributed world-wide to the homeless.

◇ **Nation:** Habitat for Humanity is an organization that builds homes for people in poorer regions of the United States.

◇ **State:** State taxes fund free medical services available to the poor.

◇ **Community:** Many local agencies collect "comfort kits" of toiletries, bus tokens, and meal and room vouchers that can be distributed to the homeless.

Provide printed resource materials on homelessness to stimulate ideas. Allow time for the participants to complete this portion of the project.

When the individual bags are completed, tape them to a wall. Invite the group to walk through the "art gallery" to learn more about ways to help the homeless. Encourage everyone to browse, read, and note interesting ideas. Then, tell each person to stand near his or her posted bag. Have the participants take turns introducing themselves by name and telling one thing that they would like others to remember about the issue of homelessness. Conclude the presentation by having the group offer spontaneous prayer for those with special needs.

FIVE

I was sick

Overview

In the gospels Jesus offers little explanation for **why** people suffer with illness. Rather than offer explanations, Jesus met illness with action. He listened to the person's story. He forgave them of their sin. He healed them of their ailment.

Christians learn from Jesus' response to illness and act accordingly. A Christian's concern for the sick takes many forms. A traditional action or work of mercy is to *visit the sick*. A person who visits the sick is a sign of the larger community's care. A person who visits the sick brings with him or her the expression of hope rooted in the good news of Christ.

As with the other merciful works, responding to the needs of the sick takes forms other than caring for physical illness. Emotional and spiritual illness permeate all ages, classes, and cultures of people today. Jesus said that those who bring comfort to individuals whose lives have been emotionally or spiritually devastated by circumstances or events will likewise be rewarded.

The activities of this chapter will help the students to act on Jesus' direction to provide care for those who are sick. "When did we see you ill?" those on Jesus' right hand asked him. And he responded, "Whatever you did for one of the least of these who are members of my family, you did it for me" (cf. Mt 25:39, 40).

Sending a Caring Message

TURN TO ME AND BE GRACIOUS TO ME, FOR I AM LONELY AND AFFLICTED.

Psalm 25:16

LEARN

Illness suffered in isolation from a caring community is a double trauma. Not only are the effects of the illness physically wearing, but a lack of contact with others can add to feelings of fatigue, loneliness, and despair. In each community many people are isolated in their homes or in an extended care center because of a physical illness or liability. Most of these people are elderly, though today an increasing number of younger people demand long-term care because of permanent disabilities due to accidents or serious illnesses like AIDS. This activity will give participants an opportunity to remind the homebound and residents of hospice or extended care that they are loved and not forgotten by making and sending cards with messages of hope and care.

LOCATE

- Typing paper, white or colored, cut to match the size of letter size envelopes
- Letter size envelopes
- Postage
- *Wonder Under*
- Pencils or pens
- Scratch paper
- Calico, gingham, or plain colored fabric
- Scissors
- Fine point permanent markers
- Iron
- Ironing board
- Large basket

ADVANCE PREPARATION

- Obtain the names and addresses of homebound people from your church community. Or, contact the activity director of a local convalescent home, rehabilitation center, or AIDS hospice and ask for the names of residents.

✎ Iron *Wonder Under* onto the back of a variety of colors or prints of fabrics. *Wonder Under* is available in craft and fabric stores and a full set of instructions is attached to each piece.

LEAD

Ask the participants to imagine what it would be like to be homebound because of an illness or physical disability. Ask: "What would be some of your needs? How would those needs be met? How would you feel separated from your friends and the community?" After enough time for discussion, have the participants brainstorm solutions to the problems introduced by the questions and responses. Summarize by pointing out that people who are homebound with an illness often become lonely and discouraged and feel cut off from other people. Read Psalm 25:16. Discuss how the psalmist represents these same feelings.

Overview the project. Explain to the participants that they are to make greeting cards to send to people who are homebound or who are living in a convalescent home or hospice. Emphasize the importance of writing messages that are cheerful, but not silly; caring, but not depressing. Give each participant the name and address of the person they will write to. Have them write a few sample messages on scratch paper and then share them with the group. Check for appropriateness. Next, explain that the front of the cards will be decorated to look like the designs have been sewn in place. Distribute scissors and a piece of fabric backed with *Wonder Under* to each participant. Ask them to cut out from the fabric decorations like balloons, flowers, hearts or letters to spell a simple word such as "hello" or "love."

Have the participants arrange the fabric cutouts on the typing paper. Use an iron (with the steam setting turned off) to iron the designs in place. The participants should use fine point markers to create the appearance of stitching along the edges of the fabric. Have them space little "stitch marks," beginning approximately 1/4 inch in length on the fabric and extending out onto the paper. The markers can also be used to draw balloon strings or to finish other necessary parts of the designs.

The message is to be written on the inside of the card. An appropriate scripture passage or poem might also be included. Have the students sign their names to the cards and address the envelopes. Place the sealed envelopes in the basket. Gather the group in a circle around the basket. Share this simple prayer based on Psalm 25:16:

> Dear God, use our messages of caring as signs of our graciousness to be gracious to those who are lonely and afflicted. Help all those who are homebound or infirmed to know that you and your family of faith remain united to them and their needs. We make this prayer in Jesus' name. AMEN.

Mail the cards individually or in one large envelope.

Identifying the Feelings

"BLESSED ARE THOSE WHO MOURN, FOR THEY WILL BE COMFORTED."

Matthew 5:4

LEARN

You won't find the definition of "heartsick" in a medical dictionary though it is an ailment that is commonly experienced by people of all ages. Heartsickness generally involves a loss; for example, the loss of a close friend who has moved or the loss of a familiar routine as at the end of a school term. Learning to express the feelings associated with heartsickness is one way in which young people can learn to grow from their experiences. In this activity the participants will explore the theme of heartsickness through the use of mime and journal writing.

LOCATE

✎ Index cards
✎ Markers
✎ Box, cigar-size
✎ Notebook paper

✎ Pens or pencils
✎ Newsprint or chalkboard
✎ Marker or chalk

LEAD

Feelings are as much a part of a person as fingers and toes, yet they are often much less obvious and need more clarification. When discussing situations involving heartsickness—a daughter angry because of her parents' divorce or a young boy lonely when his older brother goes off to college—feelings play an important role. Part of the process of dealing with the many issues related to "heartsickness" is learning to identify and express feelings. This requires practice and participation.

Gather the participants in a circle and ask each person to name a feeling; for example, "happy," "sad," "angry," "confused," or "surprised." Write each word on a separate index card and place it in the box. Next, ask one person at a time to pick a card from the box and to pantomime in silence through facial expressions and body gestures the feeling expressed by the word. Ask the others to guess the words for the feelings being expressed. Continue until everyone has had a turn.

To summarize this portion of the activity, say:

> Remember that everyone experiences feelings, and that it is important
> to identify and express emotions in order to deal with them concretely
> and constructively. One way to do this is through the use of "I"
> statements.

Explain that an "I" statement is a personal expression of feelings. ("When I lost my math book, I felt scared that I would be in trouble with my teacher" is an example of an "I" statement.)

Distribute notebook paper and pens or pencils. Tell the participants that they are to begin a journal that captures their experience of heartsickness. Remind them to use "I" statements for each entry. The entries can be based on real or imaginary situations. Write these and other similar sentence starters on a chalkboard or a piece of newsprint:

◇ A parent loses a job;
◇ A brother or sister has a serious illness;
◇ A best friend moves to another city;
◇ A new school;
◇ A grandparent dies;
◇ A pet is lost;
◇ A car accident;
◇ You are not selected for a team.

Encourage the students to try to express their honest feelings, emotions, and experiences in each entry. Tell the students that they have the option of sharing their entries with others or keeping them private. Allow some time for one-on-one or large group sharing.

Focusing on Feelings

DO NOT WORRY ABOUT ANYTHING, BUT IN EVERYTHING
BY PRAYER AND SUPPLICATION WITH THANKSGIVING LET
YOUR REQUESTS BE MADE KNOWN TO GOD.

Philippians 4:6

LEARN

Recent medical discoveries have shown how emotional stress and anxiety are connected to many physical diseases and ailments. In this activity the students will look at some possible connections between emotions and feelings and symptoms of physical illnesses. Through actions and prayer, they will remember people who struggle with both kinds of illnesses.

LOCATE

✎ Copies of Resource 5A, "Feelings Word List"
✎ Copies of Resource 5B, "Healing Prayer"

ADVANCE PREPARATION

✎ Duplicate one copy of Resource 5A and 5B for each participant.

LEAD

Read Philippians 4:4–8 to the group. Ask the participants to name negative emotions (for example, anger, fear, hatred, or worry). Ask: "What are some ways these negative emotions can affect a person's physical health?" Allow several students the chance to comment. Then, distribute a copy of Resource 5A to each person. Say:

> Draw lines to connect a negative emotion with a physical problem
> that it may cause.

Though the answers may vary, tell the students to try to use all the entries in both columns.

After all the connections have been made, assign individuals, pairs, or small groups one emotion from the list. Allow a few minutes for the students to plan how they will portray the emotion using role-play, monologue, or silent action. When they are prepared, have the group sit in a circle. Pass out Resource 5B to each person. Read the opening prayer. Then call the group or individual who was assigned "stress" to come to the middle of the circle and share their presentation of the emotion. When it is finished, they should "freeze" in place while the rest of the participants recite the prayer for stress listed on their paper. Repeat the process for each emotion. Conclude with the final prayer.

Meeting Special Needs

THEREFORE, SINCE WE ARE SURROUNDED BY SO GREAT A CLOUD OF WITNESSES, LET US ALSO LAY ASIDE EVERY WEIGHT AND THE SIN THAT CLINGS SO CLOSELY, AND LET US RUN WITH PERSEVERANCE THE RACE THAT IS SET BEFORE US . . .

Hebrews 12:1

LEARN

Persons with physical disabilities and handicaps experience many unique challenges as they undertake "running the race" of daily life. This activity will help the participants consider some of these challenges as well as possible personal responses that they can do to help people with special needs.

LOCATE

✎ Pens or pencils

✎ Index cards

✎ Newsprint or chalkboard

✎ Marker or chalk

LEAD

Ask: "How do you help other family members meet their personal needs?" Suggestions might include helping with dinner, doing yard work, reading to a younger sibling, or sharing a new skill. After the discussion ask the participants to brainstorm a list of needs of those who are physically, mentally, or emotionally challenged. For example, a blind student who is new to a school and not familiar with the campus layout, or a mentally retarded child who is asked to ride a bus to school for the first time. Write the "need" statements on a chalkboard or newsprint. Next, ask: "What is a solution for one of these needs? How could you personally respond?"

NEED CARD

RESPONSE CARD

Organize a schedule to help the boy at lunch.

NEED CARD

Wheelchair cannot fit through narrow school door.

RESPONSE CARD

Petition the school to reconstruct doorway for equal access.

Have the students work in small groups and make playing cards that list both the needs and responses in order to play a game similar to "Go Fish." The needs should be written or illustrated on one set of cards (at least eight separate need cards per group). The group should then make five different response cards for each of the needs. Tell the students to mark only on one side. To play, place the need cards face down in a pile. Shuffle and distribute four response cards to each player. Place the remaining response cards in a separate pile. One player starts by picking a need card from the pile. He or she then asks a second player for a response to that need. If the second player has a response, he or she must read it and then give that card to the first player. The first player then has a "match" and should place the two cards where all can see. If the second player does not have a response card to match the need, the first player may draw a card from the response pile. If it is a match, the first player gets another turn. If it does not match, a new player gets a turn. Tell the group to start with the youngest player and proceed clockwise around a circle.

Continue playing the game until all the cards are used. Emphasize that everyone wins when people help each other.

Creating Recipes for Healthy Living

OR DO YOU NOT KNOW THAT YOUR BODY IS A TEMPLE OF THE HOLY SPIRIT WITHIN YOU, WHICH YOU HAVE FROM GOD, AND THAT YOU ARE NOT YOUR OWN?

1 Corinthians 6:19

LEARN

An unhealthy diet and eating disorders that result from it are problems common to people who are both young and old. Many of the young people in the group will struggle with food and diet issues as they enter adolescence and young adulthood. In this activity the students will make a notebook to list definitions and potential dangers for common food and dieting problems.

LOCATE

- Paper, 8 1/2" X 11" sheets
- Pens or pencils
- Encyclopedias, textbooks, brochures, and/or other reference materials on eating disorders and problems
- Three hole punch
- Colored report folders with binders
- Magazines
- Markers
- Glue sticks or glue
- Chalkboard or newsprint
- Chalk or marker
- Duplication machine

ADVANCE PREPARATION

- Gather reference materials on eating disorders and problems from the library, a physician, a counselor, and/or local organizations and bring them to the session.

LEAD

On a chalkboard or newsprint list common eating disorders; for example:

Bulimia
Anorexia
Food addiction
Poor nutrition and
    poor food choices
Obesity

Fad diets
Laxative addiction
Improper use of diet
Manipulation of weight
    for sports teams
Yo-yo dieting

Ask the students to share information and definitions of each. Help by filling in missing details. Read the passage from 1 Corinthians 6:19. Ask: "What do these words have to do with eating habits? What is an appropriate way to use food and regulate diet?"

Assign each student one of the issues written on the newsprint. Provide paper and pens or pencils to each person. Set up a center with resource materials that all can use. Tell the students to print firmly and neatly because their research papers will be duplicated when they are finished. Each paper should include the following information:

◇ their name;
◇ the issue;
◇ a one sentence definition of the disorder or diet problem;

◇ dangers for a person who has the problem;

◇ ways to solve the problem.

As part of the solutions section, have the students make a category titled "Friend to Friend." In this space they should list things a friend could do to help a friend who is having trouble in this area. This may include such things as listen, encourage, pray, or tell a responsible adult.

When the work is completed, return to the large group. Allow each participant to share his or her report. After all the presentations are complete, collect the worksheets.

Distribute colored report folders. Provide markers, magazines, and glue or glue sticks. Instruct the students to make a cover design for their books. This could be a drawing, a graphic design, or a collage using pictures or words from magazines. "Recipes for Healthy Living" is one possible title for the book, but encourage the participants to think of their own titles. The words to 1 Corinthians 6:19 should be written on the front, back, or inside cover. When everyone is finished, ask them to share their titles and designs.

While the students are working, duplicate the individual worksheets. Set up separate piles with worksheets for each issue. Provide a three hole punch. Allow each person to collate and punch the collection of worksheets. Encourage them to keep these notebooks for future reference on this important issue.

Uplifting the Sick

ARE ANY AMONG YOU SICK? THEY SHOULD CALL FOR THE ELDERS OF THE CHURCH AND HAVE THEM PRAY OVER THEM, ANOINTING THEM WITH OIL IN THE NAME OF THE LORD.

James 5:14

LEARN

People who are injured in accidents often need an extended period of time to recover from their injuries. During this time, the accident victim and his or her family need physical, emotional, and spiritual support from the Christian community. One way for the church to help those in need is to organize and participate in a prayer marathon. This activity provides directions for a prayer marathon based on this theme. An event of this kind will help accident victims and their families feel God's presence and comfort as well as the care of the local family of faith.

LOCATE

- ✐ Poster board, large piece
- ✐ Pen or pencil
- ✐ Paper
- ✐ Copies of Resource 5C, "Uplifting the Sick Scripture Verses"

ADVANCE PREPARATION

- ✐ Contact the family of an accident victim to inform them of the plan to hold a prayer marathon for the person's intentions and to receive their permission to proceed. (To choose an accident victim to pray for, check stories in your local newspaper to find out about people from your neighborhood or church community who have recently experienced this misfortune.) Assure them that all arrangements will be taken care of and that they will not have any responsibilities for the event.

- ✐ Select a date and duration for the prayer marathon. The duration can be two or three hours, one day or evening, a twenty-four hour period, or an entire weekend. Often a communal prayer service opens or closes the prayer marathon.

✎ Reserve the church, a chapel, or another suitable place for prayer.

✎ Advertise by placing a notice in the church bulletin. Also, prepare a prayer marathon poster which gives information on the person for whom it will be held and the date, time, location, and time slots for which people can sign up.

✎ Arrange for a musician to participate in the opening prayer service (optional).

✎ Make copies of Resource 5C, "Uplifting the Sick Scripture Verses."

LEAD

Discuss the accident and the person and family for whom the group will be praying. Inform the participants of the person's condition and any specific needs. Then, read James 5:13–15 to the group. Explain that throughout the ages Christians have met together to pray for people in need. Introduce the idea of a prayer marathon. Share how a prayer marathon works. Say:

Our prayer marathon will be held __(date and time)__ at __(place)__ .
We will be planning and conducting a short prayer service, soliciting members of our congregation to pray at certain times, and pray individually and together for the people involved in this accident.

Show the prayer marathon poster. The poster should indicate the time reserved for the prayer service and time slots marked in equal increments for people to pledge to pray at either the chosen site or in their own homes. Place the poster on an easel or bulletin board, attach a pen or pencil, and display it in a place where a great number of parishioners will see it. Encourage each group member to sign up for a time for their own prayer involvement.

For the opening prayer service, invite the members of the congregation to attend. Decide how group members will be involved. If possible, arrange for a musician to participate. Have the group suggest ideas and work together to compose an opening prayer. Choose a leader to read the prayer and lead a time of intercessory prayer for the needs of the accident victim and all affected. The response can be "Lord, hear our prayer." Choose one of the scripture suggestions from Resource 5C to be read. A participant from the group may offer a reflection following the reading. Distribute copies of Resource 5C to all who take part in the opening service and individual prayer. These scripture verses can be read and reflected on during the course of the prayer marathon. A song or prayer written by a participant can be used to conclude the opening service.

The last step is to actually hold the event. Arrange for adult volunteers to supervise the church or worship room during the hours of the marathon. As an option, part of the hours of the marathon can be assigned to those who prefer to pray in their homes. Remind the group that God will bless those who are prayed for and will also bless those who live out the words of James 5:13–15.

Proclaiming the Message

FOR THE LORD IS GOOD; HIS STEADFAST LOVE ENDURES FOREVER, AND HIS FAITHFULNESS TO ALL GENERATIONS.

Psalm 100:5

LEARN

The choices made by expectant mothers and fathers can have positive or negative effects on their unborn children. This activity will explore some of the results of bad choices made by people who have children. For example, newborns whose parents abuse alcohol may be born with fetal alcohol syndrome. Babies of heroin addicts come into the world addicted to the drug and go through a painful withdrawal process which frequently has severe side effects. Children of a parent or parents who use crack are often born prematurely and must struggle to survive. Unborn and newborn babies are also affected adversely by parents who have a sexually transmitted disease. Also, lack of proper pre-natal care or nutrition by the expectant mother can have a devastating effect on the health of the unborn child. Awareness and education are important factors in making decisions that affect self and others. The participants will explore this theme by writing and delivering hopeful messages in the form of public service announcements.

LOCATE

✎ Examples of public service announcements (optional)

✎ Paper

✎ Pens or pencils

✎ Tape recorder and blank cassette tapes (optional)

✎ Video camera, VCR, and monitor (optional)

ADVANCE PREPARATION

✎ Arrange for one or more community resource persons to speak to the group about how unhealthy choices can affect the health of unborn babies.

✎ Plan to either condense the activities into one session or spread them over two or more sessions.

LEAD

Help the participants become aware of ways in which unhealthy choices related to substance abuse, sexual behavior, nutrition, and lifestyle affect unborn and newborn babies. Invite community resource persons to share information with the class. Schedule a talk by one or more individuals or arrange for a panel discussion to address this theme. Speakers could include representatives of substance abuse organizations, alcoholism councils and counseling centers, HIV/AIDS ministries, health departments, and medical professionals.

Use the information provided by the speakers to help the students write public service announcement statements that educate and inform others of the results these types of behavior can have on innocent children. Explain that public service announcements (PSAs) are aired on radio and television stations. PSAs communicate messages to the listening and viewing audiences about important topics and upcoming events. Ask the group to share examples of PSAs they may have seen or heard.

Challenge the participants to think of messages regarding the topic that should be communicated to their own community. Assign individuals or small groups to pick one or several subjects, such as heroin addiction or lack of pre-natal care, and to write public service announcements. Write at least one PSA together, for example:

"Today's choices influence tomorrow's children," "Think about their future," or "When you drink, your baby drinks too." Distribute paper and pens or pencils. Guide the group as they prepare the public service announcements.

To extend the activity, have the students take turns recording their announcements on one audio or video cassette tape. Play the tape back to the group to allow them to hear or see their work. The final version can be sent to a radio or television station or played at a church or school open house.

Ministering in Mercy

"BLESSED ARE THE MERCIFUL, FOR THEY WILL RECEIVE MERCY."

Matthew 5:7

LEARN

There are many children who suffer terminal illnesses. There are also many organizations that respond to the needs of terminally ill children in helpful and hopeful ways. Many of these organizations provide services to terminally ill children that embody the words of the beatitude "Blessed are the merciful." Use this activity to acquaint the participants with the purposes and programs of organizations and groups that assist terminally ill children.

LOCATE

- Paper
- Pens
- Envelopes
- Postage
- Felt or other fabric
- Scissors
- Glue
- Permanent markers
- Dowel rods
- Bulletin board
- Copies of Resource 5D, "Ministry in Mercy"

ADVANCE PREPARATION

- Duplicate one copy of Resource 5D for each participant.

LEAD

Explain that serious illnesses like cancer and AIDS affect children as well as adults. Emphasize that while it is distressing to think and to talk about children who will not get better, there is a positive side to the story. There are many national as well as local sources of help for chronically ill children and their families.

Distribute copies of Resource 5D. Acquaint the participants with the programs of various groups and share a brief explanation of each. Tell the participants that they will be writing to one of the groups to request more information about the services it provides.

Pass out paper and pens and ask each participant to write to one of the agencies requesting information on its policies, programs, and publications. Provide envelopes and postage and make sure that the letters are mailed.

When the materials arrive, invite the participants to make flag-shaped banners to tell the stories of the groups they researched. Place the supplies for the project within sharing distance of the participants. Felt, fabric, or paper may be used for the background of the flags. Tell the participants to cut the materials into the shape

of a pennant. Using permanent markers, have each person write on the pennant the name and logo of the group. As an alternative, this information may be cut from the literature and glued in place. Allow time for the group to design and decorate their pennants with words and pictures that describe the mission of the organization they studied. Finally, tape or glue a dowel rod to one side of each pennant.

Display the completed pennants on a bulletin board, or use them in a parade or procession.

Taking Care of the Sick

"I WAS SICK AND YOU TOOK CARE OF ME."

Matthew 25:36b

LEARN

Taking care of the sick is not a task reserved only for medical professionals. Rather, all Christians are called to share in this important ministry. Expressions of care can take many forms. Often simply making contact with a person who is ill and offering him or her encouragement is the best expression of care. In this activity, the participants will make a banner to remind their church, school, or organization of the needs of sick people in and around their community.

LOCATE

- ✎ Felt or calico print fabrics
- ✎ Glue
- ✎ Thread
- ✎ Needles or sewing machine
- ✎ Scissors
- ✎ Tape measure or ruler
- ✎ Chalkboard or newsprint
- ✎ String or yarn
- ✎ Chalk or markers
- ✎ Self-sticking address labels
- ✎ Dowel rod
- ✎ Ribbon

ADVANCE PREPARATION

- ✎ Cut a 3′ X 4′ piece of fabric, felt, or calico. Turn one 3′ side over one inch and stitch it in place to form a casing for the dowel rod.

LEAD

Ask: "What kinds of help do people who are very sick or rehabilitating from an accident need?" Possible responses are the babysitting of young children, preparing meals, or driving to the doctor. List the suggestions on the chalkboard or newsprint. Then, ask the students to share specific times and ways that they personally cared for someone who was sick. Say:

> Many people are willing to help those who are sick, but they just don't know how to begin. You will make a banner with many pockets. The pockets will be labeled with the names of people in need, using removable, replaceable self-sticking address labels. In this way the banner can be used on an on-going basis as new situations and opportunities arise.

Ask the group to brainstorm words and decoration ideas that relate to the theme of caring for the sick. You may wish to have the group include the words from Matthew 25:36b. Cut these words and symbols out of felt or calico and glue or stitch them to the top one-half to one-third of the banner.

I was sick   127

The pockets for the banner should be about 4" X 4" and attached to the bottom portion of the banner. If the backing is felt, the pockets could be cut from a variety of complementary colors. If using calico fabric, the pockets could be cut out of a variety of patterns, creating a patchwork appearance. Glue or stitch the pockets in place, spacing them evenly in rows. Place self-sticking address labels with the names of the sick people on the front of the pockets.

Write the names and specific needs of sick or infirmed people from the parish, school, or community on index cards and slip them into the pocket that is labeled with their name. When people are interested in helping, they will read the need on these cards and then sign their names if they agree to complete the suggested task. The index cards can be updated as new needs arise. Address labels can also be added or deleted as necessary.

Slide a dowel rod through the casing at the top of the banner. Tie the ribbon in place as a hanger. Attach a pen or pencil using string, ribbon, or yarn. Hang the banner in a place where people from the church, school, or organization can easily access this important information.

Portraying Health Issues

HE WENT TO HIM AND BANDAGED HIS WOUNDS, HAVING POURED OIL AND WINE ON THEM. THEN HE PUT HIM ON HIS OWN ANIMAL, BROUGHT HIM TO AN INN, AND TOOK CARE OF HIM.

Luke 10:34

LEARN

In today's society, health care costs and issues are compelling concerns. For many people, access to adequate health care is limited by the high cost of premiums, the presence of pre-existing medical conditions, or the availability of adequate supplies and equipment. In the parable of the Good Samaritan, not only did the Samaritan bring the injured man to a place where he could receive treatment, but he also paid for the care out of his own pocket. In this activity the participants will explore the subject of health care and portray some of its issues in the form of a cooperative cartoon.

✎ Paper, 8 1/2" x 11"

✎ Pens or pencils

✎ Tape

✎ Newsprint

✎ Markers

✎ Chalkboard and chalk (optional)

LEAD

Overview the many issues in health care including cost, availability, access, personnel, hospitals, allocation, lack of supplies and equipment, legislation, insurance, medicare, medicaid, pre-existing medical conditions, and employer/employee benefits. Tell the participants that they are to survey members of the congregation, families, friends, or community residents about what they consider to be the most important health care issue. They will then use the results to make a cooperative, continuous cartoon strip to depict the information that is obtained.

Distribute paper and pens or pencils. Ask the group to write the following question at the top of the paper: "What is the most important health care issue facing the country today?" Tell them the parameters of the survey group (members of the congregation, family members, friends, or people in the neighborhood or community). Have them work individually or in groups to collect responses. They may expand the interview by asking the respondents to add suggestions for how the issue might be resolved. Allow time for this portion of the activity.

Once the surveys are completed, ask the participants to share the results. On a chalkboard or a piece of newsprint, record some of the findings. Develop with the group a cartoon character who can be featured in a health care cartoon strip. Post a sheet of newsprint and involve each participant in the process of designing and drawing the cartoon figure. Invite one person to draw the face, another the body, someone else the eyes. Continue the process until everyone has had a turn and the cartoon illustration is completed.

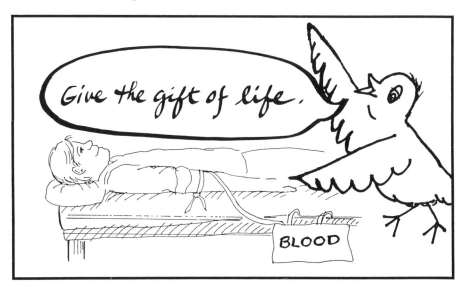

Have each participant illustrate one issue mentioned in the survey. They are to include the cartoon character in each scene (for example, the character will be attempting to receive various types of health care help). Everyone will draw his or her idea on an 8 1/2" X 11" sheet of paper. These individual sheets will become the "frames" of a cartoon. Encourage variety in the issues and topics.

As the students finish their "frames," tape the sections to the wall. When the entire cartoon is completed, ask each participant to stand by his or her drawing and explain, in turn, what they drew, as well as any information and insights they gained to address the health care issues.

S I X

I was imprisoned

Overview

Jesus' directive in Matthew 25:36 to visit the imprisoned is always a difficult one for a modern Christian. Few people know or come in contact with people who are actually detained in jail or prison. How, then, might the Christian today answer this call of discipleship?

First, the understanding of what it means to be imprisoned must be expanded. Painful experiences—for example, any form of physical, mental, or emotional abuse—can remain locked inside a person. These are a form of imprisonment. Physical ailments associated with aging or poor health can also be imprisoning. Like jailhouse bars, addictions to drugs and alcohol also take away the freedom to make healthy and wise choices. In looking at the issue of imprisonment, all these forms and more must be explored.

In this chapter the more common daily experiences of imprisonment will be introduced. The activities will also suggest ways for meeting the needs of the imprisoned with compassion and care. With God's help, each participant will be able to proclaim the words of Isaiah 61:1:

> The Spirit of the Lord God is upon me, because the Lord has
> anointed me; he has sent me to bring good news to the oppressed,
> to bind up the brokenhearted, to proclaim liberty to the captives, and
> release to the prisoners.

The participants will be able to better meet the needs of the imprisoned they encounter daily in their families, friendship groups, school, and church communities.

Spreading Some Sunshine

REMEMBER THOSE WHO ARE IN PRISON, AS THOUGH YOU WERE IN PRISON WITH THEM.

Hebrews 13:3

LEARN

Being mindful of people who have been convicted of crimes and are imprisoned in institutions is a challenge of the gospel. Also, it is important to remember the families of people who are in prison. They often suffer afflictions like fear and loneliness and the judgment of others. In this activity, the participants will suggest things that individuals and organizations can do to meet the needs of people who have family members in prison. The suggestions will be shared with the congregation on a poster that will be displayed in a prominent place.

LOCATE

- Markers, one black, one yellow, and one orange
- Construction paper
- Chalk, orange, yellow, and gold
- Bright colored 2' X 3' piece of poster board

ADVANCE PREPARATION

- Contact a prison ministry or prisoner family support organization to inquire about ways that people from your church, school, or organization might be able to assist the work they are doing.

LEAD

Discuss some of the difficulties faced by the family members of a person who is imprisoned. Ask: "In what ways are family members of people in prison also imprisoned by the experience and by the ways that they are treated by others?" List the responses with a black marker on a piece of poster board. Follow this format:

Write the words in a vertical column. If there is extra space left after the word, draw a line to the end of the page. Leave space between each word. When the list is complete, turn the poster board on its side so that the lines face up to form the impression of jail bars on the paper.

Next, use shades of orange, yellow, and gold chalk to draw circles that overlap the design and form the center of a sun depiction. Add some "sun rays" using the yellow marker. Allow each participant the chance to help with the drawing. Then, ask: "What can Christians do to spread some sunshine into the lives of people with family members who are in prison?" Allow group members to suggest as many ideas as possible. These may include:

◇ helping with child care;
◇ simple acceptance of them and their situation;
◇ providing counseling services;
◇ sharing clothing and other supplies;
◇ praying for family needs;
◇ listening to their concerns.

Using an orange marker, have the participants take turns writing the ideas on the sun rays.

Have the students choose a caption and write it on the poster board. Hang the poster in a place where others will see it. This will help them to become more aware of this requirement of discipleship and of ways to enact it. If possible, put a note in a bulletin or newsletter to let people know where the poster is and what it is about.

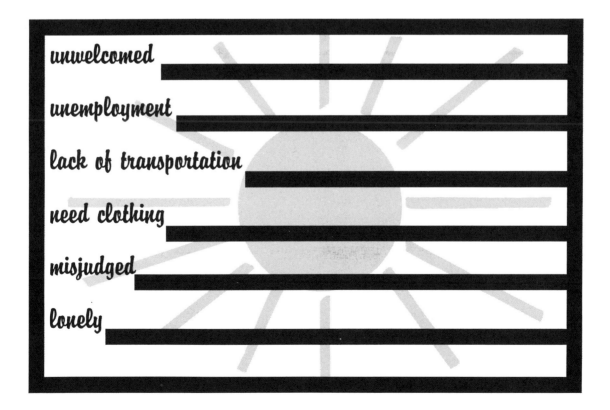

Suffering for Their Beliefs

I WANT YOU TO KNOW, BELOVED, THAT WHAT HAS HAPPENED TO ME HAS ACTUALLY HELPED TO SPREAD THE GOSPEL, SO THAT IT HAS BECOME KNOWN THROUGHOUT THE WHOLE IMPERIAL GUARD AND TO EVERYONE ELSE THAT MY IMPRISONMENT IS FOR CHRIST.

Philippians 1:12–13

LEARN

The New Testament letter of Paul to the Philippians is referred to as one of the "captivity" or "prison" letters because it is traditionally believed to have been written while Paul was imprisoned at Rome (A.D. 61 to 63) or Caesarea (A.D. 56 to 58). Suffering for a good and right cause is one of the defining characteristics of Christian discipleship. The one who suffers will often become an inspiration to others who hear about the suffering. Letters from the imprisoned to friends—as in the case of Saint Paul—link the person's suffering and the issue he or she is suffering for to others. Letters of encouragement from friends and family to the person who is imprisoned can help him or her to better endure the experience. In this activity the students will write letters that express the feelings of those who are persecuted for their beliefs.

LOCATE

- Notebook paper
- Pencils or pens
- Bibles

- Reference materials about Christians who have been persecuted for their beliefs
- Envelopes and postage (optional)

ADVANCE PREPARATION

✎ Contact Amnesty International in care of:
Amnesty International of the USA
322 Eighth Avenue
New York, NY 10001
Request written profiles of people from around the world who have been imprisoned or persecuted because of their beliefs.

LEAD

Read the passage from Philippians 1:12–13. Ask: "How can imprisonment be associated with sharing the gospel?" Point out or have the students share several current examples of people who have been imprisoned for their beliefs (for example, protestors in Tienanmen Square, South Africa, and eastern Europe). Then, divide the participants into four small groups. Distribute bibles and assign each group one chapter from the letter to the Philippians. Explain that this letter was written by Paul while he was in prison because of his Christian beliefs. Ask each group to share words or phrases that describe Paul's feelings or experiences. Also, have them locate any words of encouragement that Paul had for others. Ask one person from each group to summarize the discussion and share one or two points with the large group.

Overview the ministry of Amnesty International, a group that works to free prisoners of conscience around the world. If available, distribute materials about some of these people to each group. Then ask the participants to imagine that they have been imprisoned because of something they believe. Distribute paper and pens or pencils to each person. Say, "Write a letter that expresses your feelings about being in prison and about being persecuted for what you believe." Have the participants share their completed letters with people in their small groups.

To extend the activity, compose a group letter for someone who is imprisoned unfairly. This letter should include messages of encouragement and care. Passages from the letter to the Philippians could also be included. Make sure each person contributes at least one sentence or idea to the letter. You may wish to submit the letter to Amnesty International for publication in its newsletter.

Breaking Down Walls

FOR HE IS OUR PEACE; IN HIS FLESH HE HAS MADE BOTH
GROUPS INTO ONE AND HAS BROKEN DOWN THE DIVID-
ING WALL, THAT IS, THE HOSTILITY BETWEEN US.

Ephesians 2:14

LEARN

There are many types of cultural, economic, social, and religious walls—both figurative and literal—that imprison or separate individuals and groups from one another. These barriers take the form of things like street gangs or neighborhood boundaries, differences in language, and divisions based on economics. In this activity the participants will use Ephesians 2:14 to guide them to find ways to break down some of the unnecessary walls that have formed between groups and individuals.

LOCATE

- Shoe boxes or similar sized cartons
- Newsprint, brown paper grocery bags, or poster paints
- Tape or glue
- Brushes
- Markers or crayons
- Newspapers
- Magazines
- Scissors
- Bibles

LEAD

Read Ephesians 2:14 as an introduction to the theme. Ask the participants to list some negative emotions (for example, fear, prejudice, anger, and hate) that build walls between people. Write these in one column on a piece of newsprint. Then have the participants list positive values (for example, acceptance, understanding, peace, and love). Write these in a corresponding column.

Ask each participant to choose one negative emotion and one corresponding positive attitude from the lists. Distribute one shoe box or carton to each person. Also provide materials like paper, paints, markers, crayons, brushes, tape, glue, newspapers, and magazines. Have the participants follow these steps:

1. Cover the box with paper or paint.
2. Print the positive and the negative word on opposite sides of the "brick" with markers or crayons.
3. Add additional descriptive words and photos (either cut out from newspapers and magazines and glued in place or individually drawn).

After the bricks have been completed, have the students construct a "wall of negative emotions" by aligning the blocks so that the negative sides of the bricks face the same direction. As each piece is put in place, ask the participants to cite an example or discuss a situation of how the emotion described by the word influences people in various parts of the world. For example, people lose jobs because of fear; families reject relatives because of hurt and anger; immigration laws are stricter for people from certain countries or for those with various illnesses. When everyone has added a negative brick, allow each person to symbolically knock down part of the wall. Point out the role each individual plays in removing these emotions from their own life and circle of experience.

Finally, have the group build a pathway. The bricks should form the border of the path and the positive values should be facing up. Invite the group to walk through the pathway. Have each person pick up his or her block. Suggest that they keep these pieces as reminders to work toward breaking down the attitudes and actions that imprison or separate people or groups from one another. Gather the group in a circle and close the activity with a prayer. Ask God for the strength and help to provide a pathway to peace.

Breaking the Bonds of Materialism

FOR WHERE YOUR TREASURE IS, THERE YOUR HEART WILL BE ALSO.

Luke 12:34

LEARN

The "bonds of materialism" is a way to describe how a person can be a servant to his or her possessions and to the desire to have even more things. Many people gauge their happiness according to the size, style, and cost of things like cars, clothes, homes, and home furnishings. Oppositely, Jesus told his disciples to work for inexhaustible heavenly treasure, the kind that "no thief comes near and no moth destroys" (Lk 12:33). In this activity the participants will construct and move through a maze to remind them how easy it is to get lost in the maze of consumer messages which constantly surround people in today's society. They will also make collages depicting various material obsessions which entrap people and include alternative ideas to help people avoid this form of imprisonment.

LOCATE

- Newsprint
- Markers, one for each "dead end" of the maze
- Magazines
- Glue sticks
- Heavy 11" X 17" paper
- Cellophane tape
- Masking tape

ADVANCE PREPARATION

- With masking tape, mark a maze pattern on the floor of your meeting space. Use walls and things like easels, movable bulletin boards, large boxes, chairs, or other furniture to form "road blocks" or "dead ends." The "dead ends" serve two purposes: as actual stops along the way and as places where the individual collages the students will make can be hung. Place a blank piece of 11" X 17" writing paper at each stop. Also, provide one pen or marker at each of the "dead ends."

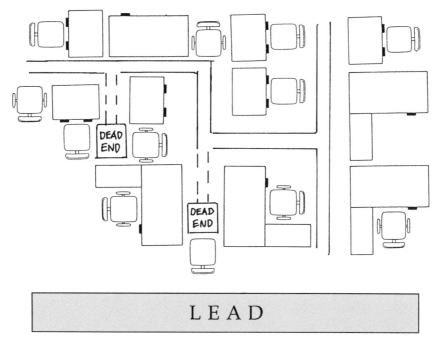

LEAD

Introduce the topic by talking about products that people want and advertisers work hard to sell. List them on newsprint, printing the names in large sizes and scattering them around the newsprint to create a chaotic appearance. Mention how overwhelming these messages can be. Ask: "How are you influenced by a radio, television, or magazine ad or commercial? Why do you think businesses spend so much money on advertising each year?"

Point out that businesses advertise in order to feed on people's desire to have things. Define materialism as "the belief that comfort, pleasure, and wealth are the highest goals or values to be attained." Ask the group to share a general profile of a person who is imprisoned by his or her desire to possess more and better things.

Assign each individual, pair, or small group to make a collage of words and magazine photos that include one of the material things that people desire (for example, automobiles or beauty products). Distribute magazines, glue sticks or tape, and background paper. Magazine ads as well as the participants' own sketches may be included on the collage. Have the students tape their completed collages on one of the "dead ends" of the maze. Make sure the art supplies are cleaned up before proceeding.

Prepare the group to go through the maze one by one. Remind them that materialism, the desire to have things, can imprison a person. Emphasize, however, that there are ways to escape the trap. People can live happily with fewer (or without) the things advertisers tell them they must have. Explain to the group members that wherever they find a collage in the maze, it is a dead end where they must stop. In order to get around that trap, they must write an alternative way of living on the paper hanging next to the collage. For example, alternatives to the automobile collage may include ideas like using public transportation, buying a used car, carpooling, and the like. Remind them that they don't have to only suggest ways to live without the items, but they can also suggest ways to feel comfortable with less of a particular product. For example, they do not have to give up buying personal and beauty care items, but they might choose less expensive brands or set a monthly budget for themselves. Also, encourage them to think of an alternative which is not already listed on the page.

After everyone has gone through the maze, gather the participants in one area. Collect the collages and the lists of alternative suggestions. Discuss the suggestions with the group, adding any ideas which were not included. Then, choose one or two volunteers to cut the collages into pieces so that each participant has at least one part. Ask the students to write on the back of their piece one way the item can imprison them and one alternative choice they can make to be free of its control. Tell the participants to take the papers home and to place them in a prominent place so that they will be reminded of the need to seek heavenly treasure over earthly treasure.

Learning about Literacy

ONE CAN INDEED COME OUT OF PRISON TO REIGN, EVEN THOUGH BORN POOR IN THE KINGDOM.

Ecclesiastes 4:14

LEARN

Illiteracy is another form of imprisonment that affects a surprisingly high percentage of adults in the United States. The inability to read, or to comprehend what is read, is a cause of unemployment or underemployment (people who can't read do not usually possess the basic skills to hold a job). Most illiterate people are economically poor; in fact the number of functionally illiterate adults corresponds to the number of people at or below the poverty level. In this session, the participants will learn more about this form of imprisonment through the use of a word game and a song-writing activity.

LOCATE

- Index cards
- Markers
- Current statistics on illiteracy
- Copies of Resource 6A, "Scrambled Word List"
- Paper
- Pens or pencils

ADVANCE PREPARATION

- Write each letter of the word I-L-L-I-T-E-R-A-C-Y on a separate index card.
- Obtain current statistics on illiteracy in the United States from the library or Literacy Council.
- Duplicate one copy of Resource 6A for each participant.

LEAD

Before explaining the theme of the session, distribute an index card containing one letter of the word illiteracy to ten different people. Say to the ten people: "Mix and match the letters and see if you can use all ten letters to form one word." If the group is able to solve the problem, have them stand in a line and display the letters in correct sequence. If they are unable to unscramble and spell the word, point out that this is how many illiterate people feel when they look at words.

Define *illiteracy* as the inability to read and write. *Functional illiteracy* is the inability to read, write, and compute well enough to perform everyday tasks such as filling out a bank deposit or reading the directions on a medicine bottle. Ask: "In what ways is an illiterate person imprisoned?" Allow time for discussion.

Distribute Resource 6A to each participant. Divide the participants into small groups and have them work together to unscramble the words or phrases. Explain that each word or phrase on the list describes a potential problem for a person who does not read well.

After an appropriate amount of time, check the answers (see below). For each, ask: "How would this item imprison illiterate people?" (For example, someone who cannot read the directions on a prescription may take or give the wrong medicine or an adult who reads at a primary level might not receive money from an insurance claim because the form was too hard to read and fill out.) Add to the discussion by citing local and national statistics on illiteracy rates, and by commenting on some of the causes of illiteracy such as learning disabilities, the cycle of poverty, and the practice of dropping out of school.

Extend this learning experience by inviting the participants to write song lyrics that explore ways in which the issue of illiteracy can be addressed. Assign or allow the small groups to choose one item from the word list, such as "medicine bottle directions," and have them work together to write lyrics to a familiar tune that suggests ways in which a person could be helped with this task. For example, the following lyrics can be sung to the tune of "Row, Row, Row Your Boat":

> Reading medicine bottle labels
>
> Is easier to do
>
> If the doctor takes the time
>
> To explain the directions to you.

Allow each group the chance to share or sing their creations with the others.

Resource 6A answers: 1. Medicine bottle directions; 2. Insurance form instructions; 3. Children's bedtime stories; 4. Street signs; 5. Maps; 6. Job applications; 7. Want ads; 8. Recipes; 9. Menus; 10. The Bible; 11. Bank slips; 12. Bills; 13. Letters; 14. Assembly directions; 15. Books; 16. Admission forms; 17. Greeting cards; 18. Bus schedules; 19. Advertisements; 20. Newspapers.

Unlocking the Fears

SOME SAT IN DARKNESS AND IN GLOOM, PRISONERS IN MISERY AND IN IRONS.

Psalm 107:10

LOCATE

According to FBI statistics a violent crime or property crime like murder, assault, forcible rape, burglary, or motor theft is committed in the United States every two seconds. As a result, common citizens have become imprisoned. Bars cover the windows of family dwellings, elderly men and women are trapped indoors after dark because they are afraid of the possibility of being attacked if they go outside, and drivers are often carjacked, that is, pulled from their cars by force while stopped at an intersection. Crime imprisons people in many ways. Though a depressing subject, exploring crime with young people is a necessity. Using the medium of photography, participants will examine the theme of imprisonment through crime and will also discover ways to empower people to respond to crime with effective actions.

LOCATE

- Newsprint or chalkboard
- Markers or chalk
- Index cards
- Scissors
- Glue
- Magazines
- Newspapers
- Cameras and film (optional)
- Paper
- Pencils or pens

ADVANCE PREPARATION

- Preview the activity. Decide which option you will use to obtain the photos or illustrations.

LEAD

Introduce the topic of crime in today's society. Suggest evidence of how crime is imprisoning (for example, home security systems, airport metal detectors, and barbed wire fences protecting property). Have the students brainstorm other items symbolic of the crime epidemic.

Once the list is developed invite the group to photograph or illustrate many of these forms of imprisonment. This can be done by organizing a field trip through the community to photograph the examples on this list. If you choose this option allow a window of time for the participants to take the photos and have them developed (instant developing cameras can also be used). Other options are to have the participants locate and cut out photos and glue them to 3" X 5" index cards or to draw their own illustrations on index cards (provide materials as needed). Regardless of the option you choose, make sure there are two identical photos or illustrations for each example. The group will play a form of the game "Concentration" with the examples they collect.

Once the photos or illustrations have been gathered, divide the participants into two teams. Shuffle the photos or cards and lay them face down on the floor or a table. Say:

> This game is called "Crime Fighters." Players from each team will alternate choosing two photos or cards and turning them over. If they match, the player is to share one way in which he or she could be a "crime fighter" and address this issue. For example, if the picture of a locked car appears, the player might suggest an escort service for the elderly. Or, a response to a picture of bars on windows or gates on doors could be to help establish a neighborhood crime watch.

Play the game in the following way: Each player may turn over two cards per turn. If they match, another turn may be taken. If they do not match, the cards are returned to a face-down position. Then the next person attempts to make a match by turning over two cards. The play continues until all pairs have been uncovered.

When the game is over, use the pictures as a bulletin board display. Provide paper and markers and invite the participants to write captions that summarize their "crime fighter" suggestions for each example.

Hiding in a Secret Prison

THE LORD SETS THE PRISONERS FREE.

Psalm 146:7b

LEARN

Elderly people may feel imprisoned for many different reasons. Physical changes, such as loss of hearing or sight, can separate an older person from full participation with others. Poverty or a fixed income can keep a person from doing all he or she would like to do. Fear of crime can trap a person inside his or her home. Other elderly people may feel confined in a nursing home where they do not choose to live. In this learning activity the group will discover ways in which some elderly people experience imprisonment. They will make soft sculpture puppets to enact some of these scenes.

LOCATE

- Nylon stockings
- Fibre fill
- Needles
- Thread to match stockings
- Straight pins
- Fabric or tacky glue
- Paper towel tubes
- Felt scraps
- Crayons or makeup
- Plastic eyes (optional)
- Fabric pieces, a variety of sizes and colors
- Yarn and/or fake fur
- Sharp scissors
- Duct tape
- 10″ X 1 1/2″ pieces of foam rubber
- Puppet stage materials (see Advance Preparation notes, below)

ADVANCE PREPARATION

- Cut the stockings into 8″ lengths.
- Construct a puppet stage using a doorway. Block off the lower section of the doorway with cardboard or a table. Tape strips of paper, fabric, or cord in the upper opening to create the appearance of bars, as in a jail cell.

LEAD

Read Psalm 146:7b–9 to the group. Ask: "How do elderly people sometimes live lives of captivity?" Allow the participants to brainstorm a list of ideas (for example, physical ailments, living in an unsafe neighborhood, loss of a driver's license, the death of a spouse). Add other ideas if necessary. Assign one of the problems that affect the elderly to one individual or small group. Tell them that they will make puppets and develop, practice, and present a puppet show based on the problem and a possible solution.

For making the puppets, provide nylon stocking pieces, fibre fill, pins, needles, thread, fabric or tacky glue, paper towel tubes, duct tape, and felt scraps to each participant. Demonstrate each of the following steps for making the puppet. Have the students follow along. Pause for clarification when needed.

1. Tie a knot in one end of the nylon piece.

2. Place a small amount of fibre fill in the bottom of the nylon punch.

3. Put a paper towel tube in the stocking.

4. Add more fibre fill, making the stocking full enough to stretch the sides of the nylon.

5. Tie a small strip of nylon around the opening so that it is closed around the paper tube.

6. Move the stuffing in various positions to create facial features. Pin temporarily in place. Use a needle and thread to sew the folds and puffs. (Remove the straight pins when done.)

7. For facial features, use crayons or makeup to shade the cheeks or areas around the eyes and mouth. Sew or glue scraps in place. Plastic eyes might also be used.

8. Use frayed fabric, yarn, additional fibre fill, or fake fur for the puppet's hair. Cut and temporarily pin in place on the nylon. Sew or glue to the nylon head and then remove the pins.

9. To form arms, cut a slit in the center of the foam rubber and slide it up the paper tube to the bottom of the head. Cut the ends of the foam into the shape of hands.

10. The puppet's clothing should be draped over the shoulders and around the neck. It can be slid up the tube by removing and replacing the puppet's arms. Sew or glue the costume in place.

The puppets are operated by holding the paper towel tube.

Allow time for the individuals or groups to prepare and practice their presentations. Each will do a short scene based on the assigned problem, showing how elderly people may feel imprisoned. Schedule time for each group or individual to present the scenes on the stage. Include a follow-up discussion segment after each presentation. Talk about people the students may know who experience the situation which was presented. Discuss ways in which the participants can help people who are imprisoned in that way.

Reading about Imprisonment

BRING ME OUT OF PRISON, SO THAT I MAY GIVE THANKS TO YOUR NAME.

Psalm 142:7

LEARN

Addictions are a form of imprisonment experienced by people of all ages. The words of Psalm 142:7 express a desire to be free of imprisonment. One way to help people avoid the imprisonment of addiction to things like drugs, alcohol, nicotine, food, and gambling is to learn more about the issues. This activity provides suggestions for holding a Read-A-Thon to help young people discover more about the kinds of addictions which can imprison.

LOCATE

- Books, magazines, journals, brochures, and comics on addiction issues
- Notebooks
- Pencils
- Snacks or meal items
- Copies of Resource 6B, "Read-A-Thon Sponsor Sheet"
- Video (optional)

ADVANCE PREPARATION

- Duplicate one copy of Resource 6B for each participant.
- Designate a non-profit ministry or organization involved in rehabilitation or prevention of one of the addictions to receive the funds collected during the Read-A-Thon.
- Have the participants collect monetary pledges for segments of reading time (for example 25 cents for each fifteen minutes).
- Enlist adult chaperons to monitor the Read-A-Thon event.

LEAD

There are many ways to inform people about addictions to things like drugs, alcohol, food, and gambling. One way is to hold a Read-A-Thon in which the participants choose and read books, journals, brochures, comics, and magazine articles that detail the various issues associated with addictive behavior. At a Read-A-Thon a block of time is chosen (for example, a twenty-four hour period from Friday to Saturday evening) and a place selected (for example your group's meeting room or the home of one of the participants). The participants commit to be present at certain times and to engage in reading materials about addiction while there. As an option, the participants may solicit donations from family members or people in the church or community for each fifteen minute time segment they are present and reading. The collected funds can be distributed to a ministry or service organization that helps addicted people.

The preparation work prior to the event is vital to the Read-A-Thon's success. At one meeting with your group, explain the idea. If the participants will gather sponsors, distribute Resource 6B, the Read-A-Thon Sponsor Sheet, to each person. Set a time and a place for the Read-A-Thon. Ask each participant to collect three separate materials on addictions and bring them along with a notebook and pen or pencil to the Read-A-Thon. If the event is to be held overnight, they will also need pillows, sleeping bags, and snacks. Inform the adult chaperons of the schedule and ask them to be present.

At the Read-A-Thon event itself, begin by explaining the procedure. Participants must spend their assigned times reading materials about addictions or writing report summaries of what they have read. Explain that you will designate breaks for snacks, exercise, videos, and the like. You may also wish to have a concluding session that allows for the participants to share the information they have learned about the imprisonments caused by addictions.

After the event, the participants are to contact their sponsors, collect the pledges, and return them to you. Arrange to send the money to the agency that you and the group have selected.

Touching with Love

HE STRETCHED OUT HIS HAND AND TOUCHED HIM, SAY-ING, "I DO CHOOSE. BE MADE CLEAN!" IMMEDIATELY HIS LEPROSY WAS CLEANSED.

Matthew 8:3

LEARN

Jesus used his hands to touch people who were ill and hurting. Jesus touched not only lepers but people who were blind, ill with fever, paralyzed, and possessed by demons. All were people who were "imprisoned" within their own bodies. Today there are also many people with physical, mental, and emotional illnesses who are imprisoned in the same way and who can benefit from the gift of touch. Use this music and gestural interpretation activity as a way of exploring the theme of touching others with the healing love of Jesus.

LOCATE

- Cassette or CD player
- Cassette tape or CD of songs with healing theme; for example: "Healing Hands" by Elton John
- Bibles
- Index cards
- Pens
- Envelopes
- Chalkboard or newsprint
- Chalk or marker
- Slides, slide projector, and screen (optional)

ADVANCE PREPARATION

- Write the words of each of the following scripture verses on separate index cards. Place the cards for each verse in separate envelopes. The verses are:

  1. Matthew 8:3 (healing the leper)

  2. Mark 5:41 (healing Jarius' daughter)

  3. Mark 10:16 (Jesus blesses the children)

  4. John 9:6 (healing the man born blind)

  5. Matthew 8:15 (healing Peter's mother-in-law)

- Write the following concluding prayer on newsprint:

  Lord Jesus, you reached out to touch and to heal people whom others shunned. Help us to follow your example by reaching out to all who are imprisoned in their own bodies, that through us they may feel your love and know the power of your healing. We ask this in your name. AMEN.

LEAD

Divide the participants into five small groups and give one envelope to each group. Explain that the words in the envelopes must be unscrambled to form a scripture passage that illustrates Jesus' attitudes and actions on healing those who are physically, mentally, or emotionally ill. After the groups have put each verse together, provide bibles so that they can check their work. Then, allow time for one or more participants from each group to share their passage and talk about what Jesus' actions meant to the person in need.

Lead a general discussion about people today who need a loving touch. Offer examples such as people with Alzheimer's Disease, HIV or AIDS, and others afflicted with various physical handicaps. Ask: "Why do you think receiving physical contact is important to people with these kinds of needs?" Invite the students to share their ideas. Point out that since Jesus is no longer on earth it is up to his followers to share his loving touch with those in need.

Play a song that expresses a message of love through the sharing of a warm touch or embrace. "Healing Hands" by Elton John is a good example. (You may also wish to show slides of people using their hands to touch or help others and coordinate the visual presentation with the song.) Play the song a second time and ask the group to add gestures to the music, reaching their hands out to one another at the appropriate times.

After the song, encourage the participants to express what it felt like to reach out and to take hold of another person's hand. Discuss ways in which this can be done on a regular basis, especially in relation to people who are imprisoned within their own bodies. If possible, arrange a visit to a hospital or nursing home and share the music and gestural interpretation with the residents who need a special touch of Jesus' love.

Display the concluding prayer script. Recite it together.

Feeling Trapped by Abuse

RETURN TO YOUR STRONGHOLD, O PRISONERS OF HOPE;
TODAY I DECLARE THAT I WILL RESTORE TO YOU DOUBLE.

Zechariah 9:12

LEARN

A person who has been abused as a child may be imprisoned by fear, anger, and sadness as an adult. Sometimes the abuse hurts so much and is so scary that the person blocks it from memory. When this happens part of the whole person is imprisoned within and the abuse is locked away as a dark secret. People who are or have been abused often feel separated from others because of the secret they hide. It is important for anyone who has been abused to receive the proper physical, emotional, and spiritual support so that they can feel whole again. In this activity the students will share their concern for those who have been abused and will work together to create a weaving of fabric that will be used to help them pray for the victims of abuse.

LOCATE

✏ Copies of Resource 6C, "Helping Someone Imprisoned by Abuse"

✏ Woven fabrics, plain colored

✏ Scissors

✏ Markers

✏ Heavy cord, ribbon, or yarn

✏ Cardboard, 2' X 2'

✏ Duct tape

ADVANCE PREPARATION

✏ Duplicate one copy of Resource 6C for each person.

✏ Follow these directions to make a large loom for weaving:

1. Locate a heavy piece of cardboard, 2' X 2'.

2. Cut a one-inch slit every two inches along each edge.

3. Using cord, yarn, or ribbon, string the loom. Start at the top left corner. Tie the cord in a knot between the end of the cardboard and the first slit. Use duct tape to tape the end of the cord firmly to the back of the cardboard.

4. Pull the cord into the first slit and then string it to the bottom of the cardboard, pulling it into the bottom slit.

5. Stretch the cord to the next bottom slit and pull it to the front of the loom.

6. String the cord to the matching slit at the top.

Repeat this pattern until the entire loom has been strung. Tape the end of the cord firmly in place, knotting it around the end of the loom for added security.

✎ Cut fabric into strips two inches wide and four to five inches longer than the width of the loom.

LEAD

Tell the group that some children experience physical, sexual, and mental abuse. That means that someone hurts their minds or bodies, or touches them in a way that hurts or scares them. Ask group members to share any knowledge they have on the topic. (This may be from news reports, documentaries, or television movies.) Correct any misunderstandings the participants may have about child abuse.

Read Zechariah 9:12. Point out that in this verse the prisoner is being offered freedom, hope, and safety. Ask the students to name things which might help a person who has been abused to feel these blessings. Also ask: "What can others do to help the abused person recover from, or be freed from, the things which he or she has experienced?" Then, distribute Resource 6C to each participant. Read and share the ideas and explanations outlined on the sheet.

Give each person a strip of cloth and a marker. If the group is large, two or three students can work together on the same strip. If the group is small, each student should be given two pieces of cloth. Each person or group should write one of the helpful words from Resource 6C on the piece of cloth. Then have the participants share in the task of weaving the pieces of cloth into the loom.

When the weaving is completed, have the group form a circle. Place the completed weaving in the middle of the circle. Distribute more cloth. Have each person hold a strip of cloth between them and the people next to them on both sides. End the activity with a shared prayer. Pray for the gifts that were written on the cloth. Conclude the prayer with these words:

HELP US, LORD, to weave these gifts into the lives of those who have been abused, helping to free them and to create for them a beautiful future. AMEN.

BIBLIOGRAPHY

I was hungry

Currie, Robin and Debbie Trafton O'Neal. *Hunger Ideas for Children*. Chicago, IL: Evangelical Lutheran Church in America, 1991.

Editors. *About World Hunger*. South Deerfield, MA: Channing L. Bete, 1987.

Hampson, Tom, Sandi McFadden, Phyllis Wezeman, and Loretta Whalen. *Make a World of Difference: Creative Ideas for Global Learning*. New York: Friendship Press, 1990.

Miller, J. Keith. *A Hunger for Healing*. San Francisco: Harper, 1991.

Office on Global Education, Church World Service and Center for Teaching International Relations, University of Denver. *Children Hungering for Justice—Grades K-4, 5-8, and 9-12*. Washington, D.C.: U.S. Committee for World Food Day.

Rupp, Joyce. *Fresh Bread and Other Gifts of Spiritual Nourishment*. Notre Dame, IN: Ave Maria Press, 1985.

Wezeman, Phyllis Vos and Jude Dennis Fournier. *Connections, Choices and Commitments: A Youth Retreat About Hunger*. Elkhart, IN: Church World Service, 1990.

I was thirsty

Editors. *Let's Learn About Using Water Wisely*. South Deerfield, MA: Channing L. Bete, 1988.

――――. *Water Conservation. A Coloring and Activities Book*. South Deerfield, MA: Channing L. Bete, 1984.

――――. *Water—Our Most Valuable Resource*. South Deerfield, MA: Channing L. Bete, 1985.

――――. Harris, D. Mark. *Embracing the Earth: Choices for Environmentally Sound Living*. Chicago, IL: Noble Press, 1990.

Hays, Edward. *Prayers for a Planetary Pilgrim*. Easton, KS: Forest of Peace Books, 1988.

Wiessner, Colleen Aalsburg and Phyllis Vos Wezeman. *The Flavors of Faith*. Brea, CA: Educational Ministries, Inc. 1990.

Wiessner, Colleen Aalsburg. *Singing Mountains and Clapping Trees*. Grandville, MI: Reformed Church Press, 1991.

I was a stranger

Fry-Miller, Kathleen M., Judith A. Myers-Walls and Janet R. Domer-Shank. *Peace Works. Young Peacemakers Project Book II*. Elgin, IL: Brethren Press, 1989.

Liechty, Anna L., Phyllis Vos Wezeman and Judith Harris Chase. *Festival of Faith: A Vacation Church School Curriculum Celebrating the Gifts of God*. Prescott, AZ: Educational Ministries, Inc., 1993.

Mains, Karen Burton. *Open Heart, Open Home*. Elgin, IL: David C. Cook, 1976.

Mummert, J. Ronald with Jeff Bach. *Refugee Ministry in the Local Congregation*. Scottdale, PA: Herald Press, 1992.

Wezeman, Phyllis Vos. *Peacemaking Creatively Through the Arts*. Brea, CA: Educational Ministries, Inc., 1990.

Wezeman, Phyllis Vos and Jude Dennis Fournier. *Joy to the World*. Notre Dame, IN: Ave Maria Press, 1992.

Wezeman, Phyllis Vos and Kenneth R. Wezeman. *Missions: 52 Creative Methods for Teaching Christ's Message*. Prescott, AZ: Educational Ministries, 1993.

I was poor

Caes, David. *Caring for the Least of These.* Scottdale, PA: Herald Press, 1992.

Cunningham, Frank J., editor. *Words To Love By . . . Mother Teresa.* Notre Dame, IN: Ave Maria Press, 1988.

Grady, Duane. *Helping the Homeless. God's Word in Action.* Elgin, IL: Brethren Press, 1988.

Kenyon, Thomas L. with Justine Blau. *What You Can Do to Help the Homeless.* New York: Simon and Schuster, 1991.

Schlabach, Gerald W. *And Who Is My Neighbor? Poverty, Privilege, and the Gospel of Jesus Christ.* Scottdale, PA: Herald Press, 1990.

Wezeman, Phyllis Vos and Colleen Aalsburg Wiessner. *Gleanings from Ruth.* Brea, CA: Educational Ministries, Inc., 1988.

_____. *Benjamin Brody's Backyard Bag.* Elgin, IL: Brethren Press, 1990.

I was sick

Archdiocese of Saint Paul-Minneapolis. *The Many Faces of Jesus, Matthew 25.* Dubuque, IA: Brown Publishing-ROA Media, 1989.

Eisentrout, Virginia A. *The Healthy Life: A Biblical Approach.* New York: United Church Press, 1989.

Hamma, Robert M. *Come to Me: Prayers in Times of Illness.* Notre Dame, IN: Ave Maria Press, 1993.

Raber, Ann. *Congregational Wellness Course.* Goshen, IN: Mennonite Mutual Aid, 1987.

Travis, John W. and Regina Sara Ryan. *Wellness Workbook.* Berkeley, CA: Ten Speed Press, 1988.

Wezeman, Phyllis Vos. *Through the Heart: Creative Activities for Learning About HIV/AIDS.* Cleveland, OH: United Church Press, 1994.

Yancey, Philip. *Where Is God When It Hurts?* Grand Rapids, MI: Zondervan, 1977.

I was imprisoned

Colson, Charles. *Born Again.* Grand Rapids, MI: Baker Book House, 1976.

Dychtwald, Ken and Joe Flower. *Age Wave: The Challenges and Opportunities of an Aging America.* Los Angeles: Jeremy P. Tarcher, Inc., 1989.

Feldmeth, Joann Ross and Midge Wallace Finley. *We Weep for Ourselves and Our Children.* San Francisco, CA: Harper, 1990.

Peck, M. Scott. *The Road Less Traveled: A New Psychology of Love, Traditional Values and Spiritual Growth.* New York: Simon and Schuster, 1978.

Washton, Arnold M. and Donna Boundy. *Willpower's Not Enough: Recovering from Addictions of Every Kind.* New York: Harper Collins, 1989.

Yost, Don. *Waiting on the Outside.* Goshen, IN: Bridgework Theater, 1983.

Zehr, Howard. *Changing Lenses: A New Focus for Crime and Justice.* Scottdale, PA: Herald Press, 1990.

RESOURCE SECTION

The following resource pages may be duplicated for individual learning activities of *"When Did We See You?"* See the specific activity plans for instructions on the use of these materials.

RESOURCE 1A
Myths and Realities

Five of the myths of hunger[1] are:

Myth #1

There isn't enough food.

Reality

The world's grain production alone could provide everyone in the world with enough calories and protein for good health. Unfortunately, because people who are hungry are also poor, the grain is not fairly or equally distributed to all nations.

Myth #2

There isn't enough suitable land for farming.

Reality

Unfortunately, much potential farm land is uncultivated or inefficiently used. In many countries with widespread hunger, a few land owners control nearly all agricultural production. Their land is sometimes used for cash crops such as cotton or coffee instead of food. In many places, only one harvest is gathered per year when there could be two or three. Other acreage is damaged by erosion and overgrazing.

Myth #3

Hunger is the result of natural disasters.

Reality

In some areas hunger can be directly traced to floods, droughts, and other natural disasters. Yet, starvation is also common in many other parts of the world where no natural disasters have occurred.

Myth #4

Growing more food will mean less hunger in poor countries.

Reality

Until a more equitable method for distributing food between rich and poor nations is established, it does not matter how much more food is grown.

Myth #5

More foreign monetary aid must be provided to the poorer nations.

Reality

Unfortunately, foreign aid is not always properly channeled or used on food staples at all.

---

1 Church World Service. *About World Hunger*. South Deerfield, MA: Channing L. Bete, 1987. Adapted with permission.
———. *Hunger: Myths & Realities*. Baltimore: Office on Global Education, N.D. Adapted with permission.
———. *Make a World of Difference: Creative Activities for Global Learning*. New York: Friendship Press, 1990. Adapted with permission.
Lapé, Frances Moore and Joseph Collins. *World Hunger: Twelve Myths*. San Francisco: Food First, 1986. Adapted with permission.

162

RESOURCE 1B
Bible Situation Cards

Directions: Duplicate. Cut on the dashed lines to separate the cards.

1. The _____ paid an innkeeper to feed and take care of an injured man until he recovered from being mugged.

Read: Luke 10:29–37

2. A widow shared her last bit of _____ and _____ with Elijah. A miracle occurred and she and her son did not run out of food for many days.

Read: I Kings 17:7–16

3. _____ gave grain and bread to his family to sustain them during a severe famine.

Read: Genesis 45:16–24

4. The disciples had fished all night without catching anything. Jesus told them to cast their nets on the other side. They caught more than the boat could hold, a total of _____ fish.

Read: John 21:4–14

5. This great leader helped the people of God celebrate the Passover with a special meal so that they would always remember how God set them free from slavery.

Read: Exodus 13:3–10

6. Boaz taught _____ how to glean the extra grain in the fields. He fed her a meal and also told his workers to leave some extra grain for her.

Read: Ruth 2:1–16

7. A young boy shared his lunch of five loaves and two fishes. Jesus used it to feed a hungry crowd of _____ people.

Read: John 6:1–14

8. Elijah was depressed and he sat under a tree and decided to die. God sent an _____ to encourage him and to bring him food.

Read: I Kings 19:1–15

9. Special servants were chosen by the first Christians to make sure the _____ were not neglected in the distribution of food.

Read: Acts 6:1–7

10. At the Last Supper, Jesus blessed bread and wine and said "Do this in _____ of me."

Read: Luke 22:19

Contemporary Situation Cards

Directions: Duplicate. Cut on the dashed lines to separate the cards.

1. Jennifer goes to a church that doesn't have a program organized to feed hungry people. It bothers her a lot. What can she do to set an example?

6. Everyone in Nikki's youth club was asked to change one eating habit that would make a small difference in combatting hunger. What can Nikki do to set an example?

2. An elderly woman on Brianna's street has a hard time getting out to the store. Brianna's mother says the woman does not eat well and also does not have much money. How can Brianna set an example?

7. Benjamin sees lots of kids wasting food every day at lunch. What can he do to make a difference and to set an example?

3. The religious education classes at Asa's church collected money to help feed hungry people. How can they use the money to help set an example?

8. Connie feels like she hears about hungry people or programs to help the poor every day. She feels guilty that she has food and others don't. There are so many things that need to be done, but she can't figure out what to do herself. How can Connie set an example?

4. Emilio's mother just had surgery and his father is very busy taking care of both his family and his job. How can Emilio's friends and classmates set an example?

9. Michael noticed that some canned food in his kitchen pantry often sits there for weeks or longer. What can Michael do to help set an example?

5. Petra was just elected to her school's student council. She wants the council to sponsor a program to help hungry people. How can she and the council set an example?

10. Thomas has always wanted to volunteer in a soup kitchen. What can he do to follow through on his idea and to set an example?

164

When I Was Hungry

"When I Was Hungry"
words and music by Joe Dowell

4. When I was hungry
   You gave me none of your bread.
   When I was weary
   You had no place for my head.
   When I was crying
   You didn't comfort me.
   You just left me to my misery.

5. We saw the hungry;
   We saw the weary too.
   We heard them crying,
   But, Lord, we didn't hear you.
   'Cause if we had, Lord,
   We would have run to your side.
   A call from the Master
   Would not be denied.

6. But when your brothers
   Cry out for help from you,
   And you turn your backs
   I feel the sorrow too.
   When your ears are deaf
   To your brother's plea,
   Your heart is hard,
   And you can't hear me.

7. When I was hungry
   You gave me nothing to eat
   When I was naked,
   No coat or shoes for my feet.
   You gave me none of your wine.
   I needed your hand,
   And you didn't have time.

CODA
How I needed your hand.
And you didn't have time.

Bread for the World
802 Rhode Island Avenue N.E.
Washington, D.C. 20018

RESOURCE 1E
Figure Patterns

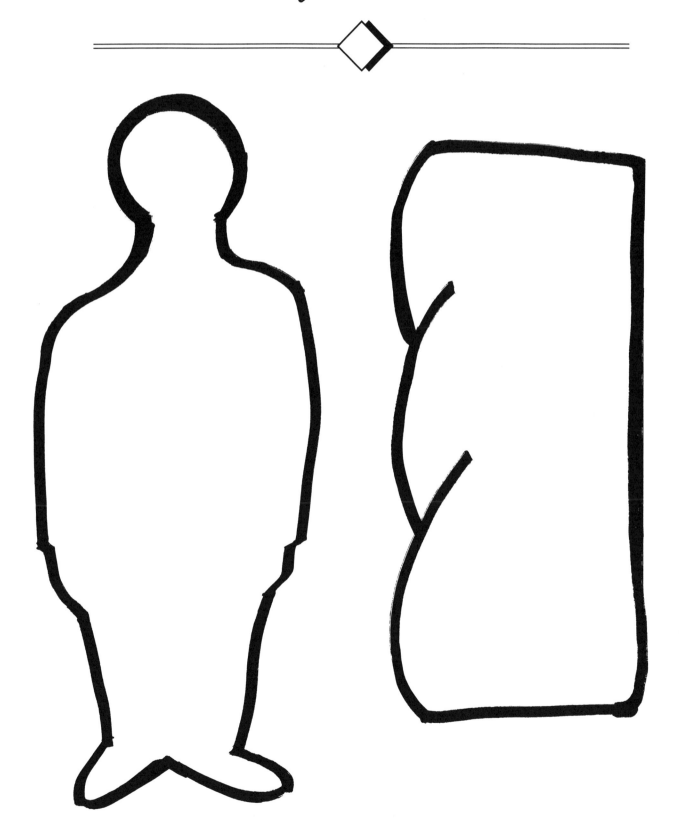

RESOURCE 1F
The Rabbit in the Moon[1]

NARRATOR

(The old man stands on a chair. Each animal bows, steps forward, or reacts as its name is called.)

Our story begins with an old man who lives in the moon. As he looked down on the earth he saw many interesting animals in the forest. He saw a monkey, a wolf, a bear, and a lion. Near the stream in the meadow at the edge of the forest he saw a lamb, a duck, and a rabbit.

The old man said:

OLD MAN

I wonder which animal is the kindest animal in the forest.

(Old man jumps off chair and stands in the circle.)

NARRATOR

The old man jumped down out of the moon, turned himself into a beggar, and walked into the forest.

Then he said:

OLD MAN

I'm hungry. I'm so hungry.

NARRATOR

When all the animals heard the old man, they said together:

ANIMALS

(Animals talk to each other.)

Let's help the old man.

NARRATOR

They talked among themselves and decided to go out and look for some good things to eat.

ANIMALS

(All the animals go to look for food. Each finds an item to give to the old man.)

NARRATOR

The old man waited patiently until all the animals returned.

Then the monkey said:

MONKEY

(Monkey walks to the man and offers him the banana.)

Konnichi Wa. (Good Afternoon.) I found you something delicious to eat. I found you a banana.

OLD MAN

(Man takes the banana.)

Arigato. (Thank you.) I like bananas.

NARRATOR

And the monkey was very pleased to be able to help the old man.

(Monkey returns to its place.)

Next the wolf came to the old man and said:

WOLF

(Wolf walks to the man and offers him the grapes.)

Konnichi Wa. I found something good for you to eat. I love grapes. These are for you.

OLD MAN

(Man takes the grapes.)

Arigato. Grapes are very good. I will enjoy them.

NARRATOR

The wolf was very glad that he could help the old man.

(Wolf returns to its place.)

Repeat and adapt the dialogue for the other animals in the play. Use other food props. Conclude with the following scene between the Old Man and the Rabbit.

NARRATOR

Then it was the rabbit's turn.

(Rabbit walks to the man.)

He came up to the old man crying. The old man said:

OLD MAN

What is the matter?

NARRATOR

But the rabbit kept crying. The old man said:

OLD MAN

What is the matter?

NARRATOR

But the rabbit kept crying. The old man said:

OLD MAN

Don't cry rabbit. What is wrong?

RABBIT

I couldn't find you anything to eat. I feel so sad.

OLD MAN

That's okay. The other animals brought me many things to eat. I will not be hungry.

RABBIT

(Rabbit offers the man sticks.)

Old man, I brought some sticks. If you build a big bonfire, rabbit meat is very delicious.

OLD MAN

(Man takes sticks.)

You, rabbit, are very kind. You mean you'd be willing to give your life to help me?

RABBIT

I would if you really needed it.

OLD MAN

You, rabbit, are the kindest animal in the whole forest. Come with me back to the moon.

(Man and rabbit stand on chairs.)

NARRATOR

Next time there is a full moon, look very carefully. You might not see a "man in the moon" but rather the face of the kind rabbit.

---

1 Pratt, David and Elsa Kula. *Magic Animals of Japan*. Berkeley, CA: Parnassus Press, 1967.

RESOURCE 1G
Multiplying the Food Rhythm Story

Leader or Group One

    People came to hear Jesus from all around.
    They came from the country; they came from the town.
    They were hungry to hear what Jesus would say,
    And crowded to be near him in every way.

All

    You can do it, you just have to try,
    And God will give the power to multiply.

Leader or Group Two

    People listened all day at Jesus' feet,
    It grew late and the folks had nothing to eat.
    To send them off hungry just wouldn't be kind,
    Jesus told the disciples to see what food they could find.

All

    You can do it, you just have to try,
    And God will give the power to multiply.

Leader or Group Three

    As they searched, they discovered one little boy.
    His five loaves and two fishes, he gave with joy.
    It surely was a very generous deed.
    But it wouldn't be all the food they would need.

All

    You can do it, you just have to try,
    And God will give the power to multiply.

Leader or Group Four

    Jesus blessed it, and broke it, and passed it about.
    The disciples thought that he would surely run out.
    Everyone there had much more than their fill,
    And believe it or not, there were leftovers still!

All

    You can do it, you just have to try,
    And God will give the power to multiply.

Leader or Group Five

    You may think that there is little you can do,
    But God will multiply your gifts and talents, too.
    You can help feed hungry people everywhere.
    And with God's help, you can show that you care.

All

    You can do it, you just have to try,
    And God will give the power to multiply.

RESOURCE 1H
Sharing Food in a Hungry World Litany[1]

Leader

The earth is the Lord's. The Lord created the world and all who dwell therein.

All

We are the people of the major continents of the world. We love life and offer praise to the Lord of our lives. Let every kindred, every tribe on this terrestrial ball, to God all majesty ascribe and crown the Lord of all.

Leader

Praise be to God, the Lord of all the peoples of earth.

Africa

We are Africa, a continent filled with beauty and promise, pain and poverty. We yearn to be free.

Asia

Burdened with masses of hungry people, we, Asia, cry for the bread of heaven and the bread of earth.

Europe

Once mighty in the eyes of the world, and now the most densely populated of the continents, we, Europe, seek economic stability.

South America

Rapidly growing in people and poverty, we of South America look to our neighbors to the north, east, and west.

North America

We are on top of the world. We in North America possess many things, and yet we are anxious about our dependence upon the exports of the rest of the world to maintain our lifestyle.

All

Praise be to God, the Lord of all the peoples of the earth.

Leader

How many of you are there on your continent?

Africa

Twelve percent of the people live in Africa.

Asia

Fifty-eight percent of the people live in Asia.

Europe

Sixteen percent of the people live in Europe.

South America

Eight percent of the people live in South America.

North America

Six percent of the people live in North America.

Leader

Do you people earn enough to have enough to eat, to eat well?

Africa

Our 12 percent of the world's people in Africa eat 8 percent of the world's food.

Asia

Our 58 percent of the world's people in Asia eat 23 percent of the world's food.

Europe

Our 16 percent of the world's people in Europe eat 36 percent of the world's food.

South America

Our 8 percent of the world's people in South America eat 11 percent of the world's food.

North America

Our 6 percent of the world's people in North America eat 22 percent of the world's food.

Leader

This unequal distribution is the cause of the malnourishment and starvation in God's world and it should be the concern of all Christians. What can we do?

All

Perhaps the nations that have more than enough food will share with those who don't have enough. Perhaps businesses can help developing countries solve their own problems by sharing technology and resources. Perhaps churches can give more to help hungry people help themselves. Perhaps we all can make decisions to help our hungry world help itself.

---

1 Church World Service Office on Global Education (Tom Hampson, Sandi McFadden, Phyllis Vos Wezeman, and Loretta Whalen). *Make a World of Difference : Creative Activities for Global Learning*. New York: Friendship Press, 1990. Adapted with permission.

Discovering Water Facts Game Cards

Cut on the dashed line. Place in the appropriate water bucket.

1.
Water Cycle
True or false? Hydro is a Greek word that means water.

1.
Water Fact
More than one million gallons of water are needed to make an automobile.

2.
Water Cycle
True or false? Water is recycled once a week.

2.
Water Fact
A cow needs three gallons of water to produce a gallon of milk.

3.
Water Cycle
True or false? Water appears in three states: liquid, solid, and gas.

3.
Water Fact
It takes fourteen hundred gallons of water to grow and process the ingredients for a hamburger, french fries, and soft drink.

4.
Water Cycle
True or false? Transpiration is the process by which plants and animals give off water vapor.

4.
Water Fact
It is estimated that twenty-five thousand people die each day at least due in part to the lack of clean drinking water.

5.
Water Cycle
True or false? All water goes through the water cycle at the same time and rate.

5.
Water Fact
Eighty percent of all sickness and disease in the world can be attributed to inadequate water and sanitation.

172

1. Water Memory

Tell about one time you had fun in water.

2. Water Memory

Share one experience of thirst.

3. Water Memory

Talk about a time water helped transport you from one place to another.

4. Water Memory

Tell about one time you needed water and didn't have any.

5. Water Memory

Describe one way you've used water for health-related purposes.

1. Water Pollution

Balloons cause danger to marine animals because the animals think the balloons are:

a. toys   b. food   c. shelter.

2. Water Pollution

Plastic rings that hold six packs of cans together should be:

a. left on the beach   b. thrown in the garbage   c. snipped before being thrown away.

3. Water Pollution

Chemical spills in oceans affect:

a. people   b. marine life   c. both.

4. Water Pollution

Fertilizers are most dangerous when they contaminate:

a. ground water   b. hands   c. bushes.

5. Water Pollution

Major pollutants in oceans include:

a. untreated sewage   b. oil   c. both.

173

1. **Water Scripture Story/Verse**
Exodus 14:1–21 (Moses and the parting of the Red Sea)

1. **Water Song**
"Raindrops Keep Falling on My Head"

2. **Water Scripture Story/Verse**
Genesis 5:1—9:17 (Noah and the ark)

2. **Water Song**
"Rain, Rain, Go Away"

3. **Water Scripture Story/Verse**
Jonah 1—2 (Jonah and the whale)

3. **Water Song**
"I've Got Peace Like a River"

4. **Water Scripture Story/Verse**
John 2:1–11 (Jesus changes water into wine.)

4. **Water Song**
"Peace Is Flowing Like a River"

5. **Water Scripture Story/Verse**
Matthew 13:17 (Jesus' baptism in the Jordan River)

5. **Water Song**
"Wide, Wide as the Ocean"

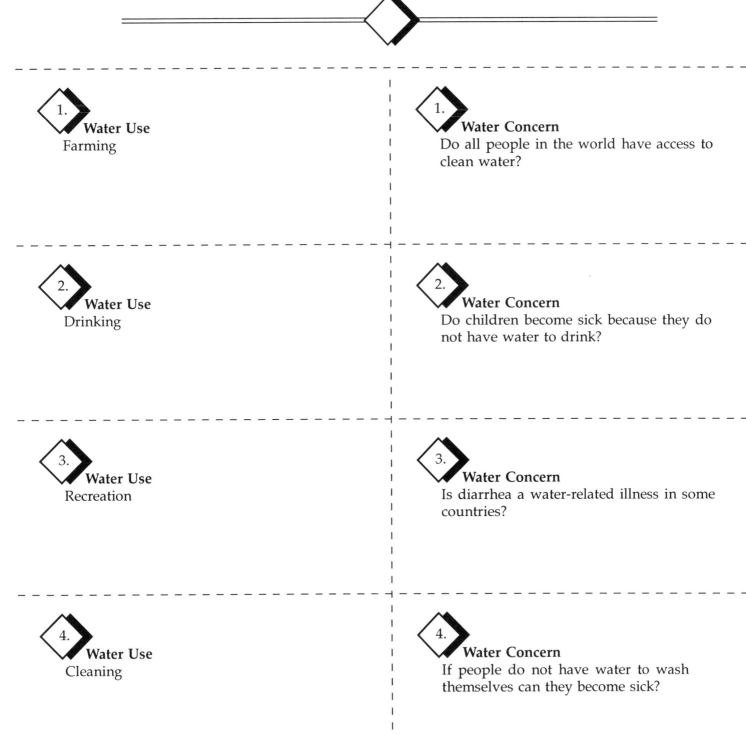

1. Water Use
Farming

1. Water Concern
Do all people in the world have access to clean water?

2. Water Use
Drinking

2. Water Concern
Do children become sick because they do not have water to drink?

3. Water Use
Recreation

3. Water Concern
Is diarrhea a water-related illness in some countries?

4. Water Use
Cleaning

4. Water Concern
If people do not have water to wash themselves can they become sick?

5. Water Use
Medicinal

5. Water Concern
Is infant death related to unhealthy water standards in some countries?

1. Water Project
World relief organizations provide tools and construction materials to dig wells in underdeveloped countries.

2. Water Project
Systems of pumping ground water to storage tanks are being developed in many countries of the world.

3. Water Project
New irrigation techniques result in increased food crops in many areas.

4. Water Project
Percolation (means "draining" or "oozing") dams filter the water into the soil below, helping to raise the water table.

5. Water Project
Fish farms are being developed to supplement the diets of many people.

RESOURCE 2B
Discovering Water Facts Game Sheet

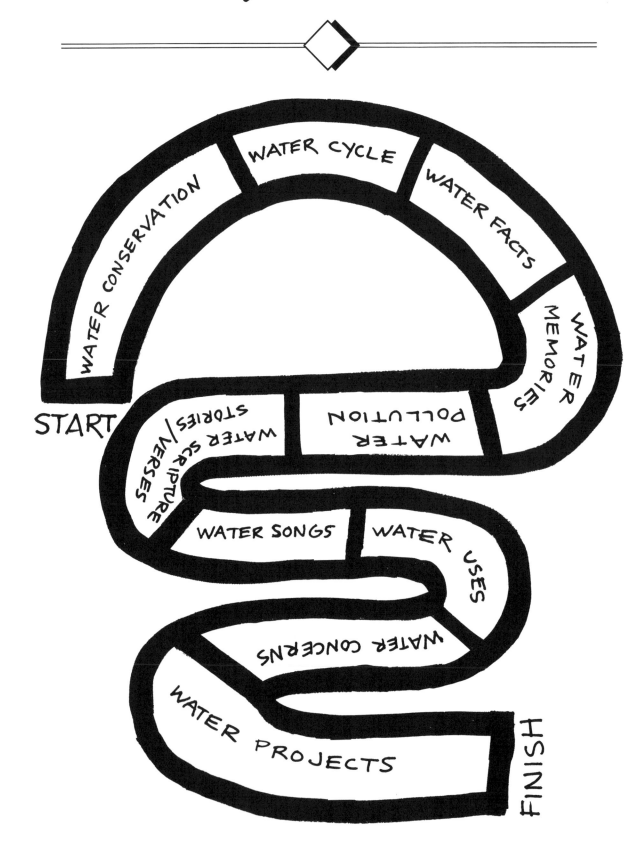

RESOURCE 2C
Scripture Verse Options

The following verses trace the theme of living water from both the Old and New Testament.

◇ Genesis 1:1–2; 9–10
◇ Deuteronomy 8:7-9
◇ Psalm 1:1-3
◇ Psalm 23:1-2
◇ Psalm 42:1-2a
◇ Psalm 65:9–10
◇ Isaiah 35:5-7
◇ Isaiah 41:17-20
◇ Isaiah 58:11
◇ Matthew 3:11
◇ John 4:7-15
◇ John 7:37-38
◇ John 13:3-5
◇ Revelation 7:15-17

RESOURCE 3A
Conflict Situations

Directions: Duplicate. Cut on the dashed lines to separate the cards.

◇ Andrew and his family use dinner time to keep from becoming strangers. Show what they do.

◇ Everyone in Brianna's family is home for the holidays. But all the kids and mom and dad are each doing their own separate activities. Show how they can spend time together and grow as a family instead.

◇ Shawnee's family asks each other questions that help them stay informed about and interested in each other's lives. For example, "How was work today?" or "What was your favorite part of the movie?" Show how they do it. Add several other questions to your presentation.

◇ Jim is with a group of friends when one of them says, "My family is like a bunch of strangers all living in the same house. We never see each other or do anything together!" What can Jim say to help his friend? Show what could be done to help.

◇ Anika and her brother have separate interests and friends. They hardly ever see each other any more. Illustrate how they can mend their relationship.

◇ Cindy's father lives in another town. She only gets to see him every other weekend. Show how she can maintain a close relationship with her father in spite of their infrequent time together.

◇ Raj's mother works the swing shift from 4 p.m. to midnight. He feels like he doesn't get to see her enough. She also feels sad, but she has to work when assigned. Show what they can say to each other about this problem and what they might do to improve this situation.

◇ Nathan had a fight with his sister. He hasn't talked to her in two weeks. Show what he could do to bridge the gap.

◇ Austin, his brother, and his parents are constantly bickering about the lack of time each boy spends at home. Show how they might be able to talk about and solve this problem.

RESOURCE 3B
Hospitality Matching Game

Directions: Match the description in the left-hand column with the correct letter of the word from the right-hand column.

Welcoming Customs

1. In Somalia guests entering a home are sprayed with sweet smelling _____.
2. Beautiful floral necklaces given to newcomers in Hawaii are called _____.
3. After eating a good meal in a Turkish home, a guest may show appreciation with a loud _____.
4. Traditional welcoming ceremonies in Russia involve breaking bread and dipping it into _____.
5. Hospitality in French homes is shown by offering visitors a selection of candies and _____.
6. When family, friends, or strangers arrive at a home in the United States, the host or hostess welcomes the guests by offering to take their _____.
7. In England the fruit that has become a symbol of hospitality is the _____.
8. "Welkommen," the German word for welcome is displayed in homes, stores, and public places on _____.

A. Chocolates
B. Burp
C. Pineapple
D. Perfume
E. Signs
F. Salt
G. Coats
H. Leis

RESOURCE 3C
Many Ways to Say Love

Take a look at these various words for love. Try to add some more to the list. Use these words to help you construct a mobile.

Language	Word for Love
Czech	Laska
Danish	Elskov
Dutch	Liefde
Finnish	Rakkaus
French	Amour
German	Liebe
Greek	Agape
Hungarian	Szeretet
Italian	Amore
Norwegian	Kjaerlighet
Polish	Milosc
Portuguese	Amor
Spanish	Amor
Swedish	Karlek

RESOURCE 3D
Scripture Riddles

Directions: Read each riddle clue. Who do you think it describes? Write your guess on the first line. Then work with a partner to look up each citation. Check your answers. Write the correct answer on the second line.

1. These two special people walked out of their tent,

    Down the road they saw strangers—angels God had sent.

    They welcomed them giving them water, food, and rest,

    Too old to become parents, with a miracle baby they were blessed.

    Guess: _____

    Read: Genesis 18:1–10

    Answer: _____

2. Tired and thirsty, Jacob spotted a well,

    A woman drew him water and let him rest for a spell.

    Then she invited him home, into her family's life,

    Later both were blessed when she became his wife.

    Guess: _____

    Read: Genesis 29:9–20

    Answer: _____

3. Elijah needed food and a place to stay,

    But these two people had only enough for one day.

    With the love of the Lord, they opened their door,

    And day after day their supplies were restored.

    Guess: _____

    Read: 1 Kings 17:8–16

    Answer: _____

4. This woman saw a holy man named Elisha passing one day,

    She and her husband gave him food and built a room for him to stay.

    Elisha asked how he could thank her for all that she had done,

    God answered Elisha's prayer for her and sent a son.

Guess: _____

Read: 2 Kings 4:8–17

Answer: _____

5. Soon to be married; happy, young, and free,
   This couple discovered God would send a stranger—a baby!
   The young woman responded, "May God be adored!"
   They became the earthly parents of Christ Jesus our Lord.

Guess: _____

Read: Luke 1:26–38

Answer: _____

6. These two sisters and a brother made Jesus Christ their friend.
   Soon they also welcomed the disciples, time together they would spend.
   They were blessed by Jesus' caring and his never-ending love,
   And when the brother sadly died, Christ sent a miracle from above.

Guess: _____

Read: John 11:17–44

Answer: _____

7. Traveling down a lonely road to Jericho,
   This man found a foreign stranger laying on the road.
   Others passed by and left him bleeding there,
   To this day this man is an example of how to care.

Guess: _____

Read: Luke 10:25–37

Answer: _____

8. Down by the river, this woman knelt and prayed,
   God answered her pleas and sent Paul her way.
   He told her about Jesus and she felt so blessed,
   She invited him to her home to share the happiness.

Guess: _____

Read: Acts 16:11–15

Answer: _____

RESOURCE 4A
Scavenger Hunt List

Complete each item on the list with your group.

1. List the names of the contact persons at two local parishes or congregations that offer support to the poor and the type of help available.

2. List three community organizations that sponsor advocacy programs. Supply the names of groups, contact people, addresses, phone numbers, and a list of services.

3. List two youth service projects designed to educate and support teen-agers at-risk. Describe the programs offered.

4. List the names and services provided by two organizations that offer support for children living at the poverty level. Describe the programs provided.

5. List the phone numbers and hours for three sites that offer after-school care. Supply information on the costs and qualifications for the programs.

6. List the meeting times and services offered by two support groups for the unemployed.

7. List the names and resources provided by two substance abuse and treatment agencies.

*8. Interview a worker at a food, clothing, or shelter location and write a short paragraph about the services provided and the work he or she does. If possible, photograph the person you interview.

*9. Collect brochures from two different agencies that offer counseling services to families living in poverty.

*10. Go to a library and record the titles of ten books on poverty-related subjects.

* Optional

RESOURCE 5A
Feelings Word List

Directions: Draw lines connecting a feeling from the left column with an illness or disease in the right column that may result from it.

Feelings	*Illness or Disease*
Stress	Headaches
Anger	Stroke
Grudge	Depression
Fear	Ulcer
Holding in Feelings	Heart Attack
Jealousy	Cancer
Resentment	Asthma
Worry	Exhaustion
Concern about the Past	Loss of Appetite
Sadness	High Blood Pressure

RESOURCE 5B
Healing Prayer

Opening Prayer:
DEAR LORD, heal our minds and emotions so that our bodies may also be whole.

For those under stress:
O LORD, be with those whose lives are overcome with stress.

For those who are angry:
GOD, bring peace to the hearts of the angry.

For those carrying a grudge:
DEAR LORD, remove unhealthy grudges from our hearts.

For those living in fear:
GOD, give your peace to those who are ruled by fear.

For those who hold in their feelings:
O LORD, bring freedom to those who are imprisoned by their own feelings.

For those who are jealous:
GIVER OF ALL THAT IS GOOD, take away the unproductive feelings of envy and jealousy.

For those who carry resentment:
DEAR GOD, please replace our resentment with joy and contentment.

For those who worry:
O LORD, help all those whose lives are bound up and lost in constant worry to be able to put their trust in you.

For those who are unnecessarily concerned about the past:
DEAR GOD, help us to accept your offer of new life.

For those who are sad:
GOD help us to feel your joy.

Closing Prayer:
DEAR LORD, heal our minds and emotions so that our bodies may also be whole. We ask this in your name. Amen.

RESOURCE 5C
Uplifting the Sick Scripture Verses

◇ Isaiah 40:30–31

◇ Luke 4:18–21

◇ Psalm 139:7–14

◇ Isaiah 43:1–3a

◇ Psalm 23

◇ Psalm 46

◇ Psalm 103:1–5

◇ Psalm 118:4–5

◇ Jeremiah 29:11–13

RESOURCE 5D
Ministry in Mercy

◇ *A Special Wish Foundation*
2244 S. Hamilton Road, Suite 202
Columbus, OH 43232
(614) 575-9474

Physicians, nurses, social workers, psychologists, attorneys, and business people work to grant wishes of children and adolescents under twenty years of age who are afflicted with a life-threatening disease.

◇ *A Wish with Wings*
P. O. Box 3457
Arlington, TX 76010
(817) 469-9474

This group raises funds and makes arrangements to fulfill wishes of catastrophically ill children for toys, trips, or introductions to celebrities.

◇ *Children's Wish Foundation International*
7840 Roswell Road, Suite 301
Atlanta, GA 30358
(404) 393-9474

This foundation seeks to fulfill the wishes of terminally ill children under eighteen years old.

◇ *Famous Fone Friends*
9101 Sawyer Street
Los Angeles, CA 90035
(310) 204-5683

Arranges for a well-known actor, athlete, or other celebrity to call a sick child.

◇ *Give Kids the World*
210 S. Bass Road
Kissimmee, FL 34746
(407) 396-1114

Provides funding for a six-day cost-free vacation for terminally ill children and their families at Walt Disney World and other entertainment complexes.

◇ *Mail for Tots*
25 New Chardon Street, P. O. Box 8699
Boston, MA 02114
(617) 242-3538

Volunteers and donors write cheerful letters to seriously ill children.

◇ *Make a Wish Foundation*

2600 N. Central Avenue, Suite 936
Phoenix, AZ 85004
(602) 240-6600

Grants the wishes of children with life-threatening illnesses in order to provide the children and their families with special memories as well as a welcome respite from the daily stress of their situation.

◇ *Ronald McDonald House*

McDonald's Corporation
Kroc Drive
Oakbrook, IL 60521
(708) 575-7418

Provides housing and hospitality to families of hospitalized children.

RESOURCE 6A
Scrambled Word List

Directions: Unscramble each word or phrase to learn a different way in which a person who is illiterate is imprisoned. Illiterate people cannot read:

1. cniedemi teotlb tenidsocri
2. unisanrec rfmo ttrssuiicnno
3. sedicnrlh metibde rsostei
4. tester nsgsi
5. pmas
6. bjo ltspaincpiao
7. tawn sad
8. csipree
9. nseum
10. eht lbibe
11. aknb positde spsil
12. slbli
13. treslet
14. msblysae tosrdcinie
15. kosbo
16. sndaiosmi rsfom
17. egrtgeni dacsr
18. ubs chedssule
19. tsdetirvmeanse
20. psenwpeasr

RESOURCE 6B
Read-A-Thon Sponsor Sheet

Dear Sponsors,

   We the _____ group are sponsoring a Read-A-Thon to better inform ourselves on the many issues connected with addictions to things like drugs, alcohol, food, and gambling.

   We are asking you to pledge a donation for the time we have promised to read. All the collected funds will be donated to:

_____

   You will be contacted after the event takes place on _____ so that you can make your donation. Thank you very much.

Sincerely,

_____

- -

_____ will read for _____ minutes about issues associated with addictions.

I agree to pledge the following amount for each minute of reading:

   Pledge   Signature

_____

_____

_____

_____

_____

_____

RESOURCE 6C Helping Someone Imprisoned by Abuse

Understanding
People who have been abused need to know that others **understand** what they have experienced.

Accepting
People who have been abused need to feel **accepted** and liked by others. They often feel "bad" or "damaged" instead.

Listening
Listening is one of the best gifts a person can give to another person. Allowing people to talk about feelings can help them heal from their sadness or anger.

Caring
Caring for someone who has been abused by showing a loving attitude and acting in kind ways helps him or her understand that the world is full of good people.

Believing
Sometimes a person tells someone else about the abuse and he or she is not believed. It is important to **believe** the person.

Responding
If you are told about someone who has been abused, **respond** by directing the person to a responsible adult who can help the person with the problem.

Protecting
If someone is currently abused, it is important to **protect** them by helping them find safety.

Supporting
Although the abuse may have taken place long before you met the person, you can help him or her by **supporting** the person during the often long healing process that must take place.

Empathizing
To **empathize** with another means to try to put yourself in the other person's situation. What if it were you who had been abused?

Sympathizing
Sometimes people who have been abused need someone to **sympathize** with them, cry with them, feel for them.

Praying
Pray for the people who have experienced abuse. You can also pray for all people who are sad or hurting because of this experience in their lives.

Laughing
Done correctly and at the right time, **laughing** can be very healing. Having fun can help a person to feel better and enjoy life again.